issues
challenges
and alternatives
in teaching
adult esl

Virginia L. Sauvé

OXFORD
UNIVERSITY PRESS

OXFORD
UNIVERSITY PRESS

70 Wynford Drive, Don Mills, Ontario M3C 1J9
www.oupcan.com

Oxford University Press is a department of the University of Oxford.
It furthers the University's objective of excellence in research, scholarship,
and education by publishing worldwide in

Oxford New York

Athens Auckland Bangkok Bogotá Buenos Aires Calcutta
Cape Town Chennai Dar es Salaam Delhi Florence Hong Kong Istanbul
Karachi Kuala Lumpur Madrid Melbourne Mexico City Mumbai
Nairobi Paris São Paulo Singapore Taipei Tokyo Toronto Warsaw

with associated companies in Berlin   Ibadan

Oxford is a trade mark of Oxford University Press
in the UK and in certain other countries

Published in Canada
by Oxford University Press

Canadian Cataloguing in Publication Data

Sauvé, Virginia L. (Virginia Louise), 1946-
Voices and visions : issues, challenges and alternatives in teaching adult ESL
Includes bibliographical references and index.

ISBN 0-19-541394-6

1. English language – Study and teaching as a second language.* I. Title.

PE1128.A2S283 2000   428'.0071'5   C99-932972-3

Cover & Text Design: Tearney McMurtry

1 2 3 4 - 03 02 01 00

This book is printed on permanent (acid-free) paper ∞
Printed in Canada

Contents

Acknowledgements

I would like to offer my sincere thanks to the following people who have supported the preparation of *Voices and Visions:*

Elsa Auerbach, Tracey Derwing, and Mary Ashworth for their comments and support on the proposal.

Employers and funders over the years whose support allowed me to develop my ideas, especially Jeet Gill, formerly of Canada Employment and Immigration Commission, and Carolyn Dieleman of Alberta Advanced Education and Career Development.

Mentors and teachers, from whom I have learned much, in particular, Tetsuo Aoki and Gordon McIntosh, whose encouragement and support in my graduate studies helped me over the rough patches.

Colleagues, teachers of English Language Professionals and Portals from whom I continue to learn, especially Azeb Zemariam, a rare individual with a rare gift as an educator.

Students, who have both taught me and warmed my heart.

Monica Schwalbe and Merrilee Brand for their excellence and dedication to editing, and Yvonne MacMillan of Oxford University Press, for her patience in missed deadlines, and Robert Doyle, also of Oxford, whose initial support made this book a real possibility (We miss you Robert!).

Phyllis Wilson for her careful attention to detail in typing the final copy of this manuscript.

The three excellent reviewers whose detailed attention to the initial manuscript made the job of editing and rewriting much easier. I especially hope that you are happy with the end product.

And my family, for their patience in supporting the long hours of writing and editing this text.

To all of you, my hearty thanks!

Virginia L. Sauvé, Ph.D.

Introduction

Voice

This is the second book in a series entitled *Voices and Visions*. Lest the reader assume that these books contain the voices and visions of many, let me hasten to say that this is not the intent. These are my voices and visions. My intent in choosing this overall title for the series is to direct our attention to two important concepts which, while being central to this field of practice, are also, I believe, sadly neglected. *Voice* is so much more than a sound coming from someone's vocal chords. Voice is about power. Those who have a strong sense of their own voice know that they can act meaningfully in the world around them and that their actions will make a difference. Those who have Voice know that they have the power to create the world they choose to live in, and to unmake those aspects of life, which they find limiting or destructive to themselves and to others.

We are uniquely privileged in ESL in particular (and as educators in general) to have a great deal of power to foster passivity or activity in those we teach. Or, to put it differently, teachers can reproduce automatons who do what they are told without question, or we can foster the learners' sense of participation and responsibility in the world. Our faith in and respect for learners facilitates their maintaining or regaining confidence in themselves in what is, for them, a new world—initially often a confusing, frightening, and depressing place. We can make our classrooms places of joy or places of painful struggle. We can learn from the learners or pretend that our knowledge is the only knowledge that counts. Valuing only our knowledge is demeaning and far from the truth, while valuing their knowledge encourages learners to remember and cherish what they know and who they are, as well as to attend to what they do not know. In addition, valuing the learners ensures that, year by year, we continue to grow in our understandings as to who the learners are, what they have to contribute to our societies, and how our world can be a happier, better place for all of us.

When we focus our lessons on grammar and vocabulary, around topics we have selected or which appear in someone's curriculum, and within timetables of someone else's making, we are not doing all we can to enable the learner's coming to voice. When we send the learner to a counsellor to solve a simple problem, or do it ourselves rather than taking the time to assist that learner to solve the problem him or herself, we may not be serving the interest of that learner in becoming self-sufficient in this society. If we are to maximize our opportunities to enable the learner to come to a strong sense of his or her own voice, we have to face our own issues of power and powerlessness. If we love teaching ESL because it makes us feel powerful, we need to examine closely whose interests we teach, and we need to make some unequivocal shifts.

Vision

Some years ago, when I was preparing to do the research for my doctorate, I did some preliminary studies to narrow my research interests. In one of these studies, I asked this question of teachers: "What is your vision of Canadian society, in particular as regards the role of the immigrant?" Most of the few respondents who were able to formulate an answer to this question said something like, "Well, immigrants provide labour for entry-level jobs that Canadians do not want to do." And that statement pretty well said it all.

Although each and every one of us born in North America came at some point from stock who came from another continent, and yes, that includes First Nations peoples too, most of us have lost the sense of our immigrant roots. "Immigrant" for many has ceased to be a neutral word describing a person who has immigrated to one country from another to become, in some sense, an indication of lower status. The mind conjures up those images of night office cleaners, sewing machine operators labouring in stereotypical sweatshops, and tanned labourers repairing our streets or maintaining our sewers. That is one vision of Canada, one which is all too common and which I find quite sad and limiting.

While those are certainly jobs that many immigrants with limited educations (and a few with excellent educations) are able to find, that is certainly not descriptive of the majority of immigrants who come to Canada seeking many other kinds of work. Our immigrant population is as varied as is our general population and more so. In my city, Edmonton, Alberta, the Ghermazians are a well-known family who came here from Iran some years ago and opened a small business selling carpets. They are now a very wealthy family who own among other things, the world-famous West Edmonton Mall with its submarines, dolphins, ice arena, wave pool and beach, bungee jumping, and numerous other attractions. This family might be said to represent the opposite end of the continuum from the typical stereotype of "immigrant." In fact, immigrants are statistically less likely to receive welfare than non-immigrants and many have a reputation for a diligent work ethic. Immigrants are business people, scientists, professionals, tradespeople, administrators, teachers, lawyers, doctors, dentists, and the list goes on. If English is not their first language, the majority of these newcomers to Canada have to study for a period of time to acquire sufficient language skills to put their other skills to use in our workplaces. One can only admire the tenacity and courage it takes to do this. These positive characteristics do not always come to mind when the stereotype does.

While the vision of society that sees immigrants as workers doing undesirable jobs is an ignorant one, it is, like so many aspects of ignorance, harmful to those newcomers who are seeking to establish themselves in a manner in which they can contribute to and be a part of a genuinely multicultural society. Those of us who have worked in ESL for many years have learned how much such people have to offer our communities. Beyond their work skills, which are many, those newcomers often bring with them ways of being that are in many cases kinder, friendlier, and more helpful and generous than our own.

We need to learn how to regain the sense of community that our ancestors had. Our immigrant members can teach us that. In a genuine community, people are not afraid of one another. They trust one another. They do not do violence to one another, and they do not escape into drugs and alcohol to forget their own pain temporarily. I like to envision a community in which a newcomer is met with eagerness and anticipation like an honoured guest. Such a guest is honoured for what he/she knows, for who he/she is, and for what he/she brings to the community. We would be eager to share what we had with this person knowing that when we needed something, it would also be there for us. We would spend time with such newcomers not only because it was our duty but also because it was fascinating and enjoyable and because we felt more fully human when we did so.

I present this vision as if it were unreal but, in fact, for many of us who have gotten to know an immigrant learner on a more intimate level, it is a reality now. I spent a week of summer vacation this year in California with a Vietnamese family whom I have known for many years. The mother of this family was my student twenty-two years ago. We became good friends and remained so in spite of their living in another part of the continent. I had a happy time there with them and so, they tell me, they did with me. I feel privileged to know this family. They are Buddhists, a fact which contributes, I believe, to the persistence, courage, and dignity which have been evident in their times of personal struggle. I have learned so very much from them. The opportunity to learn with them and share in their struggles was there, and I took it.

I cannot help but wonder how different North America would be if everyone enjoyed their immigrant neighbours the way I have enjoyed the company of my immigrant friends. Yet all too often I talk with immigrants who wonder why their neighbours do not talk with them, or accept their invitations to share a meal, or invite them back when they do accept. I find there is a great deal of fear of that which is unknown. And without taking that risk of reaching out to another, we miss so very much. Each one of us has the opportunity to break down the walls that separate those who fear newness and change. Vision begins with seeing ourselves in different realities. Without alternatives there is no choice. The moment we see alternatives, we have already begun to create that which we seek in our lives. The act of envisioning is a creative act. This is the power of vision.

Controversy

If you skim the list of chapters in the index, you will see some topics which may be controversial for you and for others. This does not mean you should avoid them. I was once accused of being racist because I chose to teach learners the principle of accountability, which says, in a nutshell, that rather than blaming others for the problems in our lives, it is more immediately beneficial to take what accountability we can, and ask what we can do to improve a situation for ourselves. I had gone to great pains to explain that racism has to be named for what it is and struggled against, but that did not stop one reviewer of that article from ignoring what I had said about racism and narrowing in on the side that recognizes the power of the individual to make things better for him or herself. The reviewer was incensed with my position.

I did not agree with her, but I do understand, to a degree, where she is coming from. She lives in Toronto, and the Black community in Toronto, as in many parts of the United States, has reached a point of great anger and clearly expresses its position. It ay be more difficult to talk about racism unless you are a person of colour. In Alberta perhaps the community is not as polarized. Nevertheless, I fervently believe that racism is everyone's responsibility. We have to learn to recognize racism, to understand the many ways it hides in our history, our language, and our social practices.

Many of the topics in this text are controversial. I have no doubt that some people will be angry with some of what I have said. I am prepared for that. Like them and like you, I have the right to an opinion, to a history that yields different opinions than those with a different history. As an educator and writer of this text, I take responsibility only for being authentic to my own experience and to being respectful of yours, whatever that may be. I do not sit in judgment of you, whatever your views, and I will not be swayed by those who would judge me without understanding my contexts. If we are to deal with controversial topics, and at some point we must, we have to risk conflict and upset. Personally, I abhor conflict and would prefer to avoid it, but I cannot be authentic to myself and avoid conflict too. I have tried, I assure you, with no success! Where you cannot agree with me, I ask at least that you be tolerant, as we must all learn to be, at the very least, tolerant of many diverse views in our societies. As teachers of ESL, I suspect we have more in common, you and I, than we have differences, and it is on that common ground that I invite you to consider my views and to articulate your own.

My Voice

Each of us of necessity speaks with a voice that gives us authority in one area but not in another. This voice is indicative of where we come from and where we have been, which is telling in its experiences or absence thereof. In order that you might have some insight into what has given rise to my views, allow me to tell you a little about myself and how I became involved in this work.

I was born in 1946 in a small city in southern Alberta, a conservative prairie city of about 33,000 people at that time. Lethbridge, while not a cosmopolitan place by any means, was populated by a largely Caucasian population that was about one-third Mormon at that time. A good number of Japanese-Canadians chose to settle in Lethbridge after the war, rather than return to those places from whence they had been uprooted so abruptly during the war. There were Hutterites living on the outskirts but doing their shopping in the city, and there were Native people, most of whom came in from neighbouring reserves for the day.

My first memory of the concept of race occurred when, at the age of six, I brought my first friend home from school. I had asked my mother if I could bring a friend home, and she had eagerly agreed to make cookies for us. I knocked at the door and my mother came to greet us. She looked stunned, and I looked behind me to see what she was reacting to. Recovering her composure, she invited us in where my friend and I enjoyed our milk and cookies. When my friend left, I asked my mother why she had seemed so startled when we arrived. Looking a little embarrassed, she said, "You did not tell me your friend was Japanese." Until that moment, I had not noticed.

This summer while visiting my friends in California, I remembered the same incident when their eighteen-year-old daughter reflected, with some sadness, on the difference between her experience of living in Canada and living in the United States. She said, "Virginia, in Canada I was just [Mary]. In California, I am Asian and I am reminded of it every day." The concepts we have of race are learned concepts and must be respected as such. If we are to make positive changes to the interracial relationships we have in our societies, we need to understand how our own and others' concepts were born and developed. Only then can we begin to envision and negotiate new and better ways of being.

I left home at eighteen and came to Edmonton to go to university. During my summers, I worked on Native reserves, in a mental hospital as a ward aide, and at a children's camp for the physically challenged as a counsellor in training. I studied French in Quebec one summer and graduated in 1967 with a B.A. in Sociology and Linguistics, and an Interim Teachers Certificate in teaching French. I married and had four children, which I raised largely alone after the eldest had turned eight.

Aside from teaching kindergarten on a reserve for two months as an undergraduate, my first experience of teaching English as a second language was in 1968 when I was offered a job teaching a night class at a local college. My students were newly arrived learners, mostly well educated and European. That was the year the Russian tanks rolled into Czechoslovakia, and that was my introduction to world politics. There was no curriculum, and the books that had been ordered for my class did not arrive for four weeks. So, for the first month, I was on my own, and that was the best learning experience I could have had. I had been trained to teach French as a second language, but those methods and types of materials seemed quite irrelevant to the needs of these men and women who were either looking for work or suffering from the degradation of doing work far below what they had done in their own countries.

In 1976, I took a full-time job teaching ESL at what was then the Alberta Vocational Centre. My students were various special needs learners from Edmonton. I spent several years there teaching wave after wave of refugees from Vietnam, Chile, Argentina, and the Soviet Union. I went back to school and received my Masters in Educational Administration and a Ph.D. in Curriculum Theory, and while at university, I taught courses in the departments where I was studying.

During my Ph.D. program I was fortunate enough to organize and teach the Korean Teacher Education Project for six years running. This was my first real experience with EFL (English as a Foreign Language), and I was able to make two trips to Korea to visit the teachers in their classrooms there and see how irrelevant for their EFL classroom was most of what we do in Canada teaching ESL. In Korea, there were, at that time, seventy students in each classroom, and the goal of teaching English in their classrooms was to do well in the final written tests so that one could gain entrance to a prestigious university.

In 1986, I was offered a position at the University of Manitoba teaching TESL, Applied Linguistics, and Heritage Language Methodology. A month after we arrived, my seventeen-year-old son was killed in an accident. At the end of the year, for family reasons, we returned to Edmonton where I resumed teaching in an "English in the Workplace" project I had begun just before I left. A year later, I opened English Language Professionals, a school which, in the ten years it operated, offered ESL for newcomers, job training programs for adult immigrant learners, as well as ESL literacy and English in the Workplace classes.

My close associate and good friend during that period was a unique and powerful woman who had come to Canada seventeen years earlier as a refugee from Ethiopia. She was a student in our first job training program, and she quickly stood out as a natural educator. I hired her at the end of the program, and there was no looking back. From my colleague, I learned about racism and about the power of ancient cultures to empower their members with integrity, courage, and steadfastness. She became my role model for critical modes of teaching—an area I had been trying to move into for years but had no role model present to guide my efforts.

At this time I run a small consulting company called Portals Educational Consulting Services Inc. We do various forms of workplace education. In addition, I do professional development work with teachers in various parts of Canada, write, and do research.

I did not set out to write my autobiography in this chapter. They say that any writing is a kind of autobiography, and I offer this summary so that when you find yourself faced with ideas quite different from your own in the chapters ahead, you may consider from where I come from. To some degree, we are made by our stories and experiences. We cannot know about things we have never been exposed to in some fashion. Likewise, we can never completely know what it is to be an immigrant or refugee if we ourselves have not had that experience. We *can* learn vicariously from our students, however, if we allow ourselves to do so.

Many of my students have called me an honorary immigrant and have marveled that I could understand so well what they were experiencing. I feel deeply honoured when they say that, knowing that, from their perspective, I have listened and I have learned. I have opened myself to being present to those whose experiences are different from my own and I am richer by far for having done so. I have struggled to find my common ground with those I teach. In my son's death, I understood loss in a new way. I am no longer afraid of death and what it holds, so I can listen and be present to bereaved persons in a way I could not have done before. Amongst refugees, bereavement is the norm.

As a single parent, I know what it is to count every penny and make conscious value choices about where to spend my money. In this way, I can understand to a degree how difficult it is for immigrants who come here with many obligations and responsibilities—but few financial resources. As a woman who attended graduate programs which were definitely structured by and for men, I can identify to a degree with those immigrant women who find their role too limited for their abilities and their dreams. As one who has known loneliness and depression, I can listen with compassion and speak with hope and faith in the future. This is the background to the voice which speaks this book.

Format

In keeping with my desire that this text be used as both a course text and a book of readings for interested teachers, I have prefaced each chapter with a short set of questions which frame the contents of the chapter. Please feel free to find your own answers to these questions. Your context is not mine. You are not me. We must have different answers and probably different questions.

At the end of each chapter, I have included an item marked "Workshop." This optional activity is intended to provide an opportunity to further explore some of the material in the chapter.

Parameters of the Text

The reader who approaches this text open to *story* as a legitimate way of embodying personal knowledge and who is open to challenge and controversy will find much of value. The reader who expects to find current academic theory integrated into opinions and stories will be disappointed. Of the three reviewers who read this manuscript, two expressed their delight at the fact that, unlike many academic works, this text was very easy to read. The third reviewer had many helpful suggestions but rued the absence of current academic theory in relation to the topics. While I have acted on many of that individual's suggestions, after careful thought, I decided not to do the extensive research that would be necessary to satisfy that individual. Each chapter includes references, and some, like Freire and Spender, are classics—as relevant today as when they were written. The intent of this text is to stimulate reflection on the reader's experiences and contexts, and I believe that examples and good questions are sufficient to do that. More importantly, I have found that the universities are, for the most part, doing an excellent job of presenting current theory in their courses. I would not presume to compete with current texts, but do want to add the voice of personal experience as a useful addition to those readings.

Organization of Chapters

The chapters are arranged under three general sections: "Teaching and Learning," "The Classroom and the Community," and "Being and Becoming a Professional." If you are taking a course, it may be that one of these sections is more relevant to your studies than the others. Or, it may be that your interest falls more actively into one category than the others. In any case, chapters should be able to stand alone or in conjunction with others in their group. So, read however your heart tells you to. Argue when you disagree. Scribble your own notes in the margin (if you are not using a library book!), and make this work your own by balancing my ideas and experiences with your own. That is as close to dialogue as we can get in the pages of a book, and it is in dialogue that we begin to extend our experiences and learn from those of others. It is my hope that my memories, experiences, ideas, and questions may stimulate your own, and that, somewhere in the mix, we may all come away from our consideration of these topics feeling more hopeful, more determined, and more clear than we did before.

Teaching and Learning

CHAPTER 1

Metaphors and Modalities

Questions to reflect upon:

- What values and beliefs underlie your teaching?
- Where and how did you learn these values and beliefs?
- What is the metaphor that best describes your own teaching?[1] Is it your chosen metaphor or one in which you find yourself not knowing how you got there?
- What are the positive and negative aspects of teaching from this metaphor?
- Is this metaphor in the interests of the learner or is it in the interests of a society that would exploit the learner for its own purposes?
- Is there an alternative metaphor from which you would choose to teach that better reflects the values you think you hold or would like to hold?

More than once, after giving a plenary address, I have been told that it was not so much that someone learned something new in what I said, as it was that they came to know what they already knew but didn't know they knew until I said it. As convoluted as that may sound, I am sure that most of you will know what I mean. Knowledge comes to us stage by stage. It is often said that we only truly know something when we are able to effectively teach it to someone else, and, as teachers, we have learned that to be true. I speak to you of metaphors in our teaching because in coming to see the metaphor or metaphors from which we teach, we can learn a lot about ourselves. In coming to understand

---

1 It may be that you have not thought of your own teaching in these terms before. If you have difficulty with this question and those which follow, it might be easier to return to them after trying the workshop activity at the end of the chapter.

ourselves better, we come to have more choices in what we do, and this is good.

I have come to value metaphors through the story workshops I have done over the years with different groups of teachers. In preparation for the workshops, participants are asked to write four stories, each of which illustrates an aspect of "lived" curriculum or learning which strikes them as significant. (I am not referring to the documents we call curriculum but rather to those "ah-ha" moments we all experience from time to time.)

A story has a beginning and an ending and contains a myriad of details that transport the reader into the experience about which the author is writing. A good story is one in which the reader believes he/she can actually feel the same feelings the author felt at the time of experiencing the events in the story. You can see the scene, hear the sounds, smell the smells, and feel the textures. The stories are submitted ahead of time, and we spend our time together analyzing them in small groups, and then as a large group, looking for the common themes. Of all the workshops I have done, story workshops have been perhaps the most popular. It is as if participants are shining a light upon their own work, as individuals and as a group, and then go away with exciting insights and new possibilities. Participants are able to shift their awareness of the commonplaces in their own teaching practice. It is typical in the small groups for everyone else in the group, except the writer, to see a connecting theme and/or metaphor in the person's stories. The story writer seldom sees it at first, but others do. Frequently one story, while appearing on the surface to be different from the other three, is actually the story that creates the *dialectic* or tension uniting them all.

It may be helpful for some readers interested in learning more about your own metaphors to pause here and do the activity at the end of the chapter before proceeding. By doing the work first, you will not be limited by the metaphors that are presented below.

Common Metaphors

Here are some of the more common metaphors that I have seen in people's writing.

1. The Mail Carrier Metaphor

This metaphor is very common and readily identifiable through words and phrases such as program *delivery,* learning *packages,* and *rates* of learning. In it, we see education or training as a carefully designed system in which knowledge can be packaged and delivered to learners. Such teaching and learning does not see the learners as participants in learning or creators of knowledge but sees them rather as recipients. In his classic work *Pedagogy of the Oppressed*, Paulo Freire referred to such schooling as *banking education.* In his metaphor, knowledge is deposited and withdrawn and becomes the currency which gives us, or doesn't give us, power in our lives. Education in this metaphor is very prescriptive: "Every prescription represents the imposition of one man's choice upon another, transforming the consciousness of the man prescribed to into one that conforms with the prescriber's consciousness." Needless to say, this kind of education is very oppressive, especially when it serves to maintain unjust social relationships in the communities in which it is practised.

These powerful phrases—program *delivery* and learning *packages*—contain deadly assumptions, values, and beliefs. They assume that we educators know better than the learner about what the learner needs to know and that our knowledge is of greater value than the learner's. They assume that we can know before we have even met a learner what that person needs. They assume that all learners are more or less alike and that learning is about information that can be delivered. They assume that there are acceptable and unacceptable rates of learning and that those who cannot conform to the acceptable rates are failures. Casualties are deemed to be acceptable.

In my experience, a learner learns best when he or she has articulated what he/she needs and wants to learn at a particular time. Furthermore, over the years in my ESL classrooms, I've come to realize that while my information is of value to newcomers, they often have other information that is of value, both to one another and to me. If the "curriculum" is so busy with my information that there is no space or time for theirs, we all miss out. In addition, information is not the sum total of learning. Learning involves such difficult and challenging aspects such as relationships, identity, working concepts, and cultural skills. I cannot assume that if a person is provided with sufficient information, she can learn what is needed to change her life for the better. I *can* assume that if a person is given sufficient respect, treated with gentleness and dignity, spoken to in truth and compassion, *and* given opportunities to acquire the information and skill she needs to advance in her chosen directions, the possibilities are good that she will do so.

We must also consider such issues as health and financial well-being. No quality of instruction will serve a person who is hungry or in acute pain. When a person lacks winter clothing in minus forty temperatures, that becomes the curriculum, regardless of what our documents say. When a man has just learned that his brother has been shot and killed, it is not reasonable to say that he has already had his allowable absences and cannot miss any more time without being expelled. When a father is helplessly awaiting the death of his ten-year-old son who has been diagnosed with leukemia, shortly after the learner began a job-training program, he cannot be considered a failure and be cut off from his financial support just because the government says those are the rules.

Learning is a magical and complex phenomenon. We do our best to turn it into a science, measuring everything, but for the learner that is not a good description of what is valued. A learner is happy with a program when he sees his life emerging in new directions because he is able to take advantage of new opportunities or to see new choices. The woman who has previously lost job after job because she always got into arguments, is set free when she realizes why she found herself repeatedly in that situation and how she can use other ways of dealing with problems when they arise. This learning does not come in a package. It cannot be planned and anticipated because each learner brings his or her own diverse set of problems. And whereas one learner might learn the needed skills in a matter of three months, someone else in a similar situation might require the better part of a year to do so.

Most ESL teachers in my experience intuitively know these things to be true and most have, fortunately, the freedom to close the classroom door, literally or figuratively, and do what needs to be done. However, these educators do not do so with a feeling of license. They occasionally are apologetic or evasive, explaining their actions to themselves by seeing these situations not as part of the curriculum but as an addition to it. There seems to be a very large gap between the theory we talk about in our classrooms and our actual practice. This is further hindered by the fact that few ESL teachers are also researchers and theorists, leaving those jobs to academics who have, in most cases, long ago left the ESL classrooms or who have, in some few cases, never spent much time in them to begin with.

This gap between theory and practise can easily be rectified by such practises as *participatory research*, or *action research*—as the Australians call it, in which teachers and learners work together with academics to research their own classrooms and theorize on the basis of that research. Not only do teachers and learners bring theory and practise into a dynamic relationship in such research, but through participating in a classroom setting, academics ensure that they stay grounded in current realities. It is heartening to see the growing number of academics who are working with practising teachers to do this kind of work.

2. The Military Metaphor
The Military Metaphor is not unlike the Mail Carrier Metaphor in its prescriptiveness and adherence to authority, but its language is even more vivid. When we find ourselves reading and/or writing about our work in terms of *target* groups, learning *strategies, deadlines, victory,*

and *defeat*; when we feel like the administrator of a program is acting like a general, the teachers like officers, and the students like obedient privates in a small army, we know we have been snagged by the military metaphor.

Let us break some of these notions down. We are very familiar with the notions of target groups and learning strategies. What, you may ask, is wrong with either? I find the best way to answer this is to put yourself into the group that is being targeted. Imagine that you have registered for a workshop, which looked interesting, and on the first night of class the instructor said to you, "We have chosen as the target group for this workshop those teachers who have shown poor performance in their conflict resolution skills." Perhaps you have no reaction to that statement. I do. I do not like the idea of being targeted. A target is suggestive of being at the mercy of the shooter, of being an object. I am not an object. I am a subject. In training programs that target a learner for his or her perceived deficits, we are preparing to "do it" to them, whether they like it or not. Who would knowingly choose to set themselves up as a target? And what if the shooter misses? What then? There are a lot of wounded ex-learners in our midst.

As for learning *strategies*, that expression appears more innocuous. What is wrong, we ask, with trying to find strategies that will better enable learners to learn what they need to learn? Let us think of the world of meaning surrounding the word "strategy." When something is strategic, it is calculated to bring advantage to one side at the cost of the other. People are set into battle against one another in win-lose relationships. Are we so blinded as to the possibilities inherent to social relationships that we cannot envision a world in which people live in win-win relationships? Even if you feel that the military origins of this word have nothing to do with its current use as careful planning towards a desired end, you may perhaps see that strategies are, like learning packages, planned ahead of time. We do not get to know the complexities of individual learners ahead of time, nor can we predict the events of their lives that may plunge them into unexpected chaos. When we have invested large amounts of our time and energy into planning learning strategies for a group of learners, it is not easy to let those go when the person or the events of the moment call upon us to do just that.

As teachers, we have seen on learners' faces when all is not well. Have we accounted for that in the moment, left it until the break, or chosen to ignore it altogether? No matter how good our strategies may seem for the majority, there will always be learners for whom they are obstructive or irrelevant. Are we to abandon or neglect those learners because they do not fit the mold? Is it not better to see our work as a response to the moment, a sense of being present to the individuals in all they bring to that moment?

3. The Sports Metaphor

I do not see this metaphor often but when I do, it is most often used by a male teacher. In this metaphor, the teacher sees himself as the *coach,* and the students as the *team.* The *goal* is clear and the *rules of play* are fixed. Whereas I really dislike the notion of educator as coach, an idea that was popularized in the eighties through the development of life skills instruction, there can be some very positive aspects to this metaphor. If the teacher is an energetic person who loves sports and loves to teach, the learners can in fact, feel that energy of play, of becoming a team, and meeting a challenge. Their daily successes are celebrated as points on a figurative scoreboard, and their daily failures are viewed as temporary setbacks to be lamented and overcome. The teacher, like the coach, sees it as his job to push the learners to their limits and thus get the most out of them. He does that however he can: encouraging, cajoling, humiliating, exploding, and praising when they do it "right." Some learners respond well to teaching from within this metaphor while others retreat into a quiet corner, hoping they will be left alone to work out problems that the teacher obviously has no understanding of.

4. The Theatre Metaphor

This metaphor is one of my favourites, being of a somewhat dramatic bent myself. In the Theatre Metaphor, we speak of the *role* of the teacher and the *role* of the learner. The curriculum is like the script, and the actors can choose to follow it or alter it considerably. It depends on the director and/or producer and the degree of flexibility and creative genius those people appreciate. The classroom becomes the stage, and the teacher sets the scene and the tone for the drama that ensues. This is a metaphor that values subtlety and does not mind the occasional melodrama—accepting it as part of the course. There is space here for emotion and for responding to emotion. This metaphor recognizes that emotion is a part of life and that without it, life is dry and flat. Tension and conflict are acceptable and a part of what is seen as normal, and it is the resolution of such tensions that advances the plot from scene to scene. And like any good actor, the teacher in the Theatre Metaphor is open to improvisation. When the curtain falls and the play has ended, the actors take their bows and move on to new roles.

Whereas I personally like much about this metaphor, one must be very careful to ensure that the script is not fixed and that all the actors can write their lines and exercise freedom of movement within it. The drama must have a sense of serendipity about it.

5. The Garden Metaphor

This metaphor is a favourite of elementary teachers and nurturing teachers who see themselves as *planting seeds* and *caring* for them over a period of time in which they will grow if properly *fertilized*, *weeded*, and *watered*. We do not often see the fruits of our labours and may or may not see them flower, but we have the confidence that our garden, well tended, will produce good fruits.

This caring, compassionate metaphor is also one that turns the learner into an object, albeit a valued object. Many ESL teachers favour this metaphor, seeing themselves as caretakers of wounded people—and indeed many learners in our ESL classrooms are indeed very wounded, as are many of us, for that matter. Such teachers are protective and motherly, sympathizing with student problems, lending a listening ear, and giving words of encouragement wherever they can. The danger in this metaphor lies in the possibility of the teacher becoming a rescuer. These are the teachers who get overly involved in the lives of their students—doing things *for* them rather than facilitating the development of the learners' own strengths and skills to do things for themselves.

If we find ourselves embedded deeply in this metaphor, it may be useful to ask ourselves in whose interest is it. Do we draw a sense of power and value from being able to help those who seem unable to help themselves? Do we inadvertently prolong that helplessness because helping makes us feel good?

6. The Economy (or Money) Metaphor

The Economy or Money Metaphor is a favourite of governments whose politicians and employees have a tendency to define everything in terms of what it costs. Because many of us work for the government, many of us have been snagged by this metaphor too. The Money Metaphor plans educational programs on the basis of the learner having *deficits*. One learner may have a deficit in language skills while another has a deficit in literacy. The focus is not on what the learner knows, who she is, or what she is capable of, but rather on what the learner does not know and what he or she can or cannot do. Such programs are concerned primarily with cost-effectiveness and efficiency and find casualties acceptable and inevitable. Timelines are based on the length of time a group of learners would normally take to acquire the information and skills, which have been mandated by the authorities, and programs are funded, for the most part, on the basis of who can do it the cheapest and the fastest. Teaching staff are chosen on the basis of paper credentials because it is easier and faster to hire staff on that basis than to take the time to figure out which teacher has the best qualities to enable the learners to learn what they both need and want to learn. Lines of authority are clear and largely not open to question. The government or other funder maintains control by threatening to withdraw funding if the guidelines are not followed or the goals not met in the prescribed matter. Evaluation is done using tools that can register computer-generated numbers. No one working from this metaphor is likely to be interested in case studies or whether or not lives were changed for the better because of the program. Such inquiries would be considered an inefficient use of time, money, and resources.

7. The Hospital Metaphor

Similar in some ways to the Garden Metaphor, the Hospital Metaphor places the teacher in the role of health care practitioner: *diagnosing* what is needed, *treating wounded learners*, *prescribing remedies* that work, *feeling the pulse of the classroom* to gauge its overall state of wellness, and generally conducting classes from the sense that he or she knows how to define wellness and illness. As with most of our metaphors, the learner is objectified, and his well-being is very much in the hands of the expert teacher who knows what is best. Rather than experiencing learning as an adventure, the learner becomes painfully aware of what he or she does *not* know. For the learner, this is not unlike experiencing an illness and following the doctor's directions for getting well.

I see this metaphor as a natural extension of the marriage between linguistics and psychology, which has characterized much TESL theory in the eighties and beyond. Prior to that time, much of our TESL theory came to us from Linguistics, a discipline primarily concerned with the structure of the language, and from Applied Linguistics, which was concerned with, among other things, how one acquires those structures. To be without the structures of a language in a culture that is interdependent with them—is to be handicapped. Psychology asserted itself in examining the factors of adjustment one makes in leaving all one has known and then trying to adapt and integrate into a new culture with new rules. For the first time, we began to read about the role of self-esteem in learning. Psychologists are, like doctors, professionals whose role it is to assist people to attain good health, in this case mental and emotional health. In combining linguistics and psychology as our theoretical basis for understanding the *pedagogy/andragogy* (education of adults) of ESL, it is not difficult to find oneself professing to understand what is going on for the learner and taking charge of that person's course of "treatment."

Depending on the degree to which the teacher, like the doctor or psychologist, takes charge or informs, and lets the learner take charge, this metaphor can be more or less positive or negative.

8. The Journey Metaphor

This is perhaps my favourite metaphor because the teacher becomes a sojourner on a learning journey with other pilgrims. In this spiritual metaphor we see ourselves—teacher and learner—on some sort of journey or another, seeking that which we take to be the Holy Grail. For some, it is freedom, for others material well-being, for others a loving community. Based on respect for all persons regardless of race, gender, culture, or any other difference, in this metaphor we travellers travel the roads of life together, sharing what we have, asking for what we need, and showing compassion for those along the way who appear to be struggling.

No person is regarded as better or worse than any other, although we feel more comfortable in the company of some than others. Individuals are expected to set their own destinations and to travel at a pace which is comfortable to them. No one takes it as his or her right to determine someone else's journey or to hasten them on their way. For some sojourners, the journey is more important than the destination, and each step offers its own joys and causes for celebration: getting to know a new soul along the way, celebrating diversity amongst the travellers, stopping to assist someone whose vehicle has broken down, sharing food together with what little each has brought to the table, discovering a detour more beautiful than the pre-chosen path, and stopping to smell the flowers along the way. No one thinks to evaluate the journey of another, for there is no reason to do so.

Lest this seem like a romantic notion, contrary to the realities of government budgets and accountability measures, this metaphor nonetheless offers us some alternatives with which we may begin to envision the kinds of metaphors we could be working within.

In Summary

An infinite number of potential metaphors exist. I have described only some of the more common ones I have seen. In doing so, I have tried to identify some of the values, assumptions, and beliefs inherent to those metaphors. These descriptions are offered to enable you, the reader, to hold a mirror to your own practise so that you can determine whether any given metaphor is consistent with what you value and whether it reflects the best of your capacity. I invite you to take what fits and leave what does not.

Workshop Activity

If you would like to get a better idea of the metaphor or metaphors from which you teach, and the hidden values, assumptions, and beliefs that undergird your teaching, write four stories, each one about something that strikes you as significant in relation to what it means to learn. A story has a beginning and an ending and is full of details that make it easy for the reader to enter into your experience. Do not, in the writing of the stories, analyze your experiences or pass judgments on the people or events within the stories. Let the stories speak themselves. Simply relate the sequence of events within each story.

When you have completed your stories and feel happy with them, leave them for a few days and then re-read them, this time with an eye to looking for expressions which come from some readily identifiable field of experience: banking, the military, the mail service, the theatre, etc. Circle them in your writing and see if you can find any patterns. If a word or phrase jumps out at you and you do not know why, underline it or draw an arrow in the margin beside it. *It is calling your attention for a reason.* Try to find a theme that connects your stories in some fashion. If you have trouble doing this work on your own stories, try getting together with three or four others who have done the same exercise. It is usually much easier to see these things in others' stories.

One last word of caution: the metaphors are simply mirrors that help us to see into our own individual and collective experiences with greater depth. Each metaphor can have both positive and negative aspects to it, and most of us have two or more that will appear. In relation to myself, I can see in my work through the years aspects of all of the metaphors described above.

Note to course instructors: If you assign this exercise to a class and some people find themselves coming up empty in the analysis, it may be that they have edited any indicators out of their writing in an attempt to avoid any potential criticism. Their stories will often tend to be quite flat. Try to reassure them that this is an exercise in discovery and that it is no one's place to judge anyone. Under no circumstances should one grade such an assignment, unless it is a pass-fail assignment dependent solely on doing the work to the best of one's ability and participating in discussion.

CHAPTER 2

Teaching the subject and the Subject

Questions to reflect upon:

- What takes priority in your teaching: the subject or the Subject? Does the time allotted to each support that view? Do your decisions about curriculum support that view?
- Which is more important to the majority of your students: getting the language correct or feeling safe and comfortable when speaking it?
- Do you think your students feel predominantly respected, challenged within reason, and capable of doing what they need to do, or do many feel discouraged, stupid, and incapable of learning this difficult new language?
- Do you think your students primarily see themselves as passive recipients of knowledge or active creators thereof? How do you know?
- Is the language being learned in your classroom of primary relevance to the actual contexts the learners will enter upon after leaving the classroom (e.g., type of work, community)?
- In your experience, what have been the most significant factors in determining whether or not a learner will be successful in learning the language and making her way in the community?
- In your experience, have you had the information and support you needed to do what, in your heart of hearts, you believed you needed to do in the classroom? If not, how do you account for that?

One great tension which faces every teacher is the tension between teaching a subject, such as ESL, and a Subject—a flesh-and-blood human being in all his or her uniqueness. It seems that the human mind has difficulty holding both those thoughts in balance and, at best, it seems to flip from one to the other in our teaching practise. Keeping them in balance can only happen, first, when we learn to recognize what belongs where, and secondly, when we consciously choose where our priorities lie and understand our choices.

The subject of ESL

ESL is a recognized body of knowledge and skills that has developed fairly recently if compared to traditional subjects of study such as history or mathematics, which have been taught for centuries. Not so long ago, languages were studied formally in order to translate texts and documents when one was doing research. Thus, the emphasis was on reading and writing, and that led to grammar and vocabulary as being the primary objects of study. Languages, however, have been learned informally for centuries; they were learned when people found themselves having to interact with people in different languages and in different contexts. It is not uncommon for illiterate people in many countries of the world to speak several languages that they have learned to function in the marketplace. Within the second half of this century, ESL has developed as a field of practice with recognized components: listening and speaking, reading and writing, grammar, vocabulary, and pronunciation. Because the field is still quite new and very dynamic, I believe it is still very much open to question and challenge.

Even in the thirty years I have been engaged in ESL practice, there have been many advances in our thinking. When I began teaching, the emphasis was still very much on grammar. The assumption was that if a person understood how the grammar of a language worked and had sufficient *lexicon* (vocabulary), he or she could successfully function in that language. The emphasis was very much on *form* at that point. Then, in the seventies, we moved into an emphasis on language as *function*. We were concerned with *how* the language was used. Our curricula shifted accordingly to functional and thematic curricula. Instead of the learners memorizing grammar rules and assuming that they could apply those in any situation, we began to teach them language for specific situations: a doctor's office, a parent-teacher interview, or a job interview.

Then some theorists such as Gail Moscowitz started to pay attention to the relationship between self-confidence and language learning ability. The emphasis had shifted from studying the language itself to studying how language was acquired, and it is not much of a stretch to recognize the value of having a healthy self-confidence in the often embarrassing circumstances of learning an additional language. This and other related concerns gave rise to the *communicative competence* school of thought that moved beyond form and function into examining the broader and more complex system of communication. British theorists such as Candlin, Breen, and Brumfit, and Americans such as Krashen refocused teachers on a larger picture of communication which involved relationships, worldview, and agency. We started to pay more attention to who learned well under what conditions. One of the results of this thinking was the recognition that learners who had a sense of their own choices, tended to do better than learners who were passive recipients of pre-planned programs.

Parallel to this thinking, radical educators based much of their work on that of Paulo Freire, the critical Brazilian literacy educator who had already begun to create ways for learners, both adults and children, to become Subjects rather than Objects in the classroom. The focus of these radical educators was on power. They facilitated the learners in naming their own realities—things that were important to them—and in envisioning how they would like their realities to change. Language was understood to be the medium in which human beings created their reality. It was dynamic rather than passive, and this understanding was reflected in the curriculum of *critical* teachers. Such teachers are not *transmitting* identified content so much as they are *facilitating* a process of working with learners to create a desired reality within the medium of language. A well-known example of such an educator in the United States is Elsa Auerbach. In Canada, Deborah Barndt is a widely read critical educator.

This summarizes where our ESL theory has gone over the past thirty years, but it does not begin to describe what has gone on in our class-rooms. While teachers appreciated the changing variety of available resource texts and workbooks, at the same time they have generally always done their best to respond to the real needs of the learners as they understood them, regardless of what materials they had or what the curriculum spelled out. For example, learners wanted to know what was acceptable and unacceptable in social situations. They wanted to know about the laws of the land, about the resources that were avail-able to them in terms of employment, healthcare, education, and consumerism. They wanted to know about changes to immigration and sponsorship laws in their new country. All of these topics fall under the general rubric of *settlement education* and, alongside the settlement agencies, ESL practitioners have done their best to respond to these needs as they become aware of them.

Few teachers, however, have had the inclination, the skill, or the permission to deal with larger issues of power for immigrant learners. It is a fact that many immigrant learners work in unjust workplaces where working conditions are poor if not downright illegal, and wages are minimum and insufficient to support families. As a result of this and the fact that many immigrants are also supporting family members back in refugee camps and/or in impoverished countries of origin, many such families have all adult members working not just one but two or even three jobs in some cases. Such learners are unlikely to speak out against abuse in the workplace or to become active in unions which fight for better wages and benefits for their members. These learners may be afraid of such involvement, given their histories, or they may be just plain tired and have no energy left for that kind of struggle.

As educators, we frequently come across these inequities and injustices, especially if we do workplace education. We then have to ask ourselves how our curricula need to respond to these realities. In my view not only should rights and responsibilities be part of most ESL curricula but there should also be the opportunity for the learners to learn the communicative skills needed to stand up for their rights appropriately. Too often our classrooms have encouraged passivity in learners, expecting them to obediently follow the teacher's direction, even when they experience the content as irrelevant or boring. I have walked past the doorways of far too many classrooms where the teacher was speaking and the learners were leaning on their desks, looking tired and bored. To me such a sight indicates that the learners assumed that their participation was neither welcome nor necessary.

We and most teachers in the public systems have lived with the myth that there is no place for values in the classroom, that our teaching should be objective and neutral. Our students are seldom fooled into believing this because they easily see where our values come into conflict with their own. When we choose to include *this* but not *that* in our curricula and our texts, we are acting from values, whether those values are conscious or not. When we choose to be authoritarian rather than participatory in our classrooms, believing that the teacher knows best, we are acting out of values which say that our knowledge is more valuable in this context than that of the learners, and we know better what they need than they themselves do. Without necessarily knowing it, we are teaching obedience and passivity.

In deciding what should be included in any given course of studies, we need to know a lot about the lives of the learners who are studying: Will they be working? Where will they be working? With whom will they be interacting? What do they know already? What information do they need about the language, about the community, about taking care of themselves, and about available resources? Will it be important for them to speak correctly? To write correctly? Will it be important for them to understand a variety of accents or just "broadcast" English? What will they need to read when they leave the program? Will they be able to continue to study? And most of all, no matter how well we have planned, there has to be space to make changes in our curricula when the actual students come into our classrooms. Each person is unique. And time brings us unexpected changes.

The Subjects

The Subjects in our classrooms have incredible diversity. They differ from one another in language, culture, race, religion, gender, age, health, employment skills, education, personality, status, history, social class and the experience of trauma. Is it any wonder that we have based our curricula and materials on the subject rather than the Subjects?

Recently, one of my daughters, a good friend, and I had a most insightful conversation. My daughter is a printmaker and my friend is a semi-retired professor with a strong philosophical bent. We were discussing a print she had done recently; a diptych more abstract than not. My friend asked my daughter what period of art she felt this print was from, after some discussion they agreed that it was "post-structuralist." Suddenly, my friend said something like this: "The truth of our being is not here nor there but in the space between." He was speaking of the space between the two sides of the print and also of the space between the art object and the viewer.

But when he said that, I was suddenly cast into that marvelous space between a teller's telling of a story and a listener's hearing, and I realized the profound truth of this statement in relation to education (especially to the education of persons of very diverse cultures). In a story, the meanings we hear are a union of the images cast by the teller in our minds and hearts, and the images we project from our own experiences upon those images. It is in the place where those two sets of images meet that we experience the story. Likewise, when we teach, the learner's experience lies somewhere between the teacher's words and her own experiences, which she projects as memories out to meet those words. This is one reason we so often have misunderstandings and miscommunications. Either the speaker has not given enough information for the communication to be unambiguous and stand alone, or the listener's projections have been sufficiently interfering, blocking out some aspect of what was said. Therefore, listening and reading are creative acts, as are speaking and writing.

As educators, we are, or rather we should be, accounting for these differences all the time. Any curriculum document is necessarily incomplete because we cannot know everything which is significant to know about a person when we have not met or spent considerable time with her. Our curriculum plan must be based on generalities and allow for flexible choices within a range of probabilities. We become conscious of the deficiencies in our curricula when a new "wave" of learners descends upon us. Suddenly, we find that activities, resources, and indeed ways of teaching that worked very well with one group, fall totally flat with another.

I remember teaching Chilean refugees in the seventies and enjoying their love of music and rhythm. We found that singing, jazz chants, and pronunciation classes were very popular with these students. Music enhanced their learning. Then, the Vietnamese "boat" people came in the eighties. These Vietnamese and Chinese-Vietnamese learners did not find these ways of teaching as appealing as the Latin Americans had. They tolerated them but did not get into them in the same way. It was time to change the curriculum to meet their more reflective ways of being. The illiterate men and women in that group, however, seemed not to be learning from any of the usual approaches—until one day we discovered that they seemed to learn more during the coffee breaks than they did during the classes. We designed a whole curriculum for them based on their ability to learn in relatively unstructured social settings, and it proved to be effective.

A few years later came the Eastern Europeans—Russians, Poles, Romanians, Hungarians. They were a "no-nonsense" group with very clear expectations as to what they wanted to learn and how they expected to learn it. Mostly well-educated men and women, they wanted spelling lists, grammar charts, vocabulary quizzes, and tests. They wanted to be pushed and demanded that we do so. Once again, the curriculum changed.

I have my own ideas, as I am sure you do, as to what is "good" and "not good" in a curriculum, but those ideas are of no value whatsoever if the learners in a class do not share them, or are not at least open to them in some fashion. The first principle of teaching is to start where the learners are and build from there. That, I have learned to do. I have found that if I respect a group's way of learning and give them what they want, they in turn will relax and let me introduce a few ideas of my own. It is a give-and-take situation, and that is as it should be, for we are both participants in a classroom. We simply bring different kinds of expertise to the teaching-learning situation.

Education

We cannot minimize the importance of recognizing the implications of diversity in our classrooms. Perhaps the most powerful difference of all has to do with education: how much a learner has had and how it has taken place. Well-educated learners generally have solid, successful learning strategies. It makes sense to use these strategies as much as possible, insofar as they are not in conflict with the learning ways of other learners in the class.

Most of us have had the unpleasant experience of having one group of students who want to learn this way, while another group wants to learn that way. Sometimes one group tries to impose their way on everyone—a typical scenario in a group with several people from one culture. I far prefer well-mixed classrooms, ethnically-speaking, to classrooms dominated by one culture because even if there are only three or four learners in that culture, if they are dominating, they can make life miserable for everyone.

It is significant how much education a person has had. In my experience, nothing is more difficult than trying to teach educated and uneducated learners in the same class. Even if their initial language skills are at the same basic level in English, these students are at totally different places in their approach to learning.

It took me a considerable amount of time to learn how to work with illiterate students. I could not identify with them. I had difficulty finding their starting places. It was foreign for them to sit in one place for hours at a stretch. It was foreign to hold a pencil and make markings with it. I was used to living in a world of symbols, and they were not. I did not know how to help people learn when they could not write things down. These learners needed classes of their own and a very different approach to teaching them English. Once I figured that out, I began to really enjoy working with such learners. They did not come with many fixed expectations and were open to all sorts of learnings. I have had great pleasure working with literacy learners.

Health

Health is another big factor, particularly if you are working with people who are in chronic pain. Newcomers to a country may have a backlog of health issues and no money to deal with them when they first arrive. When someone has a toothache and needs a root canal but cannot pay for it, no amount of wanting to learn can enable that individual to remember what is happening in the classroom. He needs his tooth fixed and that is that. Or, another common ailment is the chronic pain experienced by the worker with many years in Canada who suffered a back injury on the job and has been dependent on the system ever since. He lacks the resources to pay for the kinds of therapies that would give him relief, and having to sit in a classroom adds to the torment of this injury.

Other students suffer from serious depression and are on heavy medication. If they do not actually fall asleep in the classroom, they are unlikely to remember much of what has been presented and practised. Such students are not going to learn many language skills or other content until they find their way off the medication. Some of us have the energy and skill to make that happen. Others among us need to find counsellors who can work with these individuals on such problems.

The tendency for teachers who have learners with serious health problems in their classes is to bemoan that fact but see nothing they can do about it. I believe that this is an error in our thinking. Not only can we do our utmost to help the student deal with the health problem, but when there is a pattern here, we have to take our responsibility as professionals to point out those patterns to those with the authority both to do something about preventing their recurrence and to find better solutions for those who have the problems now.

Take work injuries, for example. Many injuries are caused by workers who do not have sufficient language skills to follow directions, verbal or written, or who are working long hours in multiple jobs at minimum wages (to earn sufficient income for their families here and elsewhere). This is a social problem. It is also a problem of the system when people are sent to school when they have more primary needs such as work, income, healthcare etc., which need to be met before their learning needs can be addressed. Our governments, both the civil servants and the politicians, are only aware of these situations when the public makes them aware. Because we are working with a temporarily disenfranchised population, it is not reasonable to expect them to advocate on their own behalf. We have to do it for them, and co-operate with immigrant-serving agencies whose mandate it is, in part, to do the same thing. We can do this as professional associations, as organizations, and as individuals.

Financial Situations

Financial stability is critical to learning. When a person does not have enough money for his basic necessities and for his family, it stands to reason that he is not as open to learning, and yet, many of our students are in this situation. If they are unemployed, they want to find work, perhaps part-time when they are in school and full-time when they have finished. Their minds are on this task, and if our curricula can assist them both in preparing themselves for work and in finding and maintaining it, we will have their full, undivided attention. It is crucial for language programs to have sufficient support staff to spend time sorting out financial difficulties when they arise and, to connect learners to those who can resolve their financial burdens. (Or, we need to work together with the settlement agencies who do have the staff and programs to do this work.)

On the other hand, it is a waste of resources to teach employment issues to mothers who are in English classes just to learn enough English to take their children to the doctor or dentist, or to talk to their children's teachers in the school, or to learn how to read recipes for Canadian and American food (when their older children start rejecting their ethnic foods). These women know reading is important and would like to be able to read storybooks in English to their children. If at all possible, it is good to have classes just for these mothers, with childcare included.

Gender

In Canada, we were fortunate to have had a group of civil servants in Ottawa a few years ago who recognized the importance of providing special classes for women. These classes took into account that many women come to us from cultures that are very oppressive to women, and that many women with young children cannot take advantage of existing English classes unless babysitting and transportation are provided. When the federal LINC (Language Instruction for Newcomers) programs were born in the early nineties, women were a recognized group and as such they were able to get funding for such services across the whole country. Now that LINC is winding down and the provinces are taking over ESL for newcomers, we can only hope that the provinces will maintain this awareness by continuing funding for these programs.

Gender plays a big role in the mixed classroom. It is well-documented that within our own English-speaking cultures, men tend to dominate mixed gatherings, and that is probably even more true in ESL classrooms which tend to reflect cultures more patriarchal than our own. Women tend to make way for men and to take care of them in mixed gatherings. This may appear as women remaining silent while men speak, acknowledging their comments generously, laughing at their jokes, or deferring to men when open-ended questions are asked. As educators, we need to be mindful of these realities in ensuring that each learner gets her "airtime" in the class. For those who are interested in learning more about this topic, I recommend Dale Spender's book, *Man Made Language*. Another resource is Jane Thompson's *Learning Liberation: Women's Response to Men's Education*. While there are more current references available on this topic, I have yet to find any that make the points any better. You may also want to look at *You Don't Understand: Women and Men in Conversation* by Deborah Tannen.

If you teach ESL for a period of time, you are going to have abused women in your classes. In fact, if you are an experienced ESL teacher, you have had abused women in your classes. Have you recognized them? Have you been able to be supportive of them? Do you know how to protect yourself from husbands of learners who see your intervention as harmful to their families and threatening to their power?

Abuse is a fact which crosses all boundaries: ethnic, class, economic, and religious. While abuse is more accepted in some cultures than in others, it exists everywhere, and if you have taught for two years or more and never met an abused woman, I would hazard to guess that you need to find different ways of recognizing abuse, and to give victims space to talk to you. The first and most obvious signs are bruising, cuts, or broken limbs, particularly if there seems to be a pattern of injuries continuing over time. Most women will have a story if you question them: I fell down the stairs; A door fell on me in a fire; I tripped over a carpet. And, of course, sometimes this is true. But often it is not. I had one student who came to class black and blue. Her story was she got injured by crashing a race car that weekend. It was so amazing that I believed her, and it was years later when I learned that her husband had threatened to kill her if anyone found out the truth.

Abused women do not need our sympathy or horrified reactions. They need our strength, and they need information. In all my classes I teach about women's shelters and how to access them, and about the laws in regard to spousal and child abuse. I keep confidences when women decide to share their stories with me unless they involve children. I tell students that I am ethically obligated to report any instances where a child is being abused or neglected. It is with sadness that I say I can do nothing when a woman decides to stay with an abusive husband. It is not easy for a woman who speaks little English, has no education or job skills, and has no family here to support her, to leave her husband or partner. But it is her decision, not mine to make. Whereas I generally do not give my phone number to students, I do give it to women who have discussed abuse with me, so that they know there is someone to call, in addition to the police, if they need to.

You need to be aware that giving out information about spousal abuse and taking an active role in assisting someone to seek assistance can pose a hazard. While driving one woman and her children to a shelter, I was pursued across the city by her husband. (He had gone to the school after the police assisted us in taking the baby from the home and was waiting for us when we came out with the older children.) Needless to say, he was very angry with me. Other men have also expressed their displeasure with my teaching this information, accusing me of trying to break up families.

Even when women do go to the shelters, not all have the resolve to leave abusive relationships. Many women are too frightened and feel too alone and incapable. All we can do as teachers is ensure that people know their rights by our laws and that they know what resources are available to support them should they choose to exercise those rights. We can also continue to be supportive, regardless of what decisions they make.

Status and Social Class

While most of us are fully aware of the categories I have mentioned to date such as gender and educational backgrounds, many of us have been less mindful of the influence of status and social class in the ESL classroom or have not known what to do with it when we are aware of its import. In my experience, I have tended to explain differences in people by their culture or their personality, and discerning between the two has been enough of a challenge to prevent me from seeking other explanations. However, I have had a few experiences, which hit me over the figurative head, where I could not ignore social class and status as significant factors in understanding and responding to learners.

I have observed that when status and class are signaled by some other indicator common to our culture such as occupation, many teachers automatically change their demeanour towards that individual. If a student says he is a doctor or she is a prima ballerina, one can often see the teacher's attitude shift as the teacher acknowledges what she sees as the superior qualities of that person.

However, there are many immigrants who had very significant positions of power in their countries but whose dress and current feelings of helplessness do not signal to us in any way the respect they held in their own countries as business people or community leaders, for example. Such individuals often experience difficulty accepting being "immigrants" in their new country—a title which tends to confer a rather low status in the eyes of many in their new community. Whereas I believe it is important to respect every individual regardless of who he or she is, I also try to keep a few extra drops of compassion for the person who experiences that she has lost more than those around them by immigrating here. (Chapter 11 looks specifically at social class, status, and the ESL classroom.)

Race and Ethnicity

In researching the area of race and ethnicity, I found that while American theorists tend to focus on race by discussing issues around racial discrimination and diversity, Canadian authors are more inclined to discuss them in terms of ethnicity. The writing in this chapter reflects both of these vantage points.

Many white-skinned individuals believe that the notion of race should just disappear, that there would be no interracial conflict if we just ignored race altogether. Regardless of what position one takes on that thought, people of colour currently do experience exclusion and negative treatment due to their race. Furthermore, many people of colour have developed a very distinct community or communities within their race, and they do not want these communities to be ignored. They simply want all races to be respected and accepted for who and what they are.

Because the vast majority of ESL teachers are white, middle-class women (and if you doubt that, as one reviewer did, take a look around at any large TESL conference in the country), race is a concept which is often ignored in the classroom. When racial issues arise, they are quickly swept aside. In that our job is to prepare learners to be successful in a multicultural society, and in that race is experienced as a barrier to many of the learners we teach, I do not believe we can ignore race in either our curricula or in our daily interactions with learners.

The first challenge for educators is to become sensitive ourselves to issues, which we may not have personally experienced. I have been fortunate to have worked with a very conscious Black colleague and friend. Traveling with her has been particularly enlightening. We find that our destination plays a significant part in determining how people react to us, a White and a Black woman traveling together. The most dramatic experience was in Atlanta where in one five-hour afternoon of looking, we could not find another mixed-race pair sharing one another's company—shopping, dining, or appearing to be together. We found that very peculiar.

In addition, people reacted differently to each of us. Black people acknowledged my friend with a smile or hello and treated me as if I were invisible. Some White people stared at us, others ignored us, and some even glared at us. An older Black woman watching us, chuckled merrily and shook her head as if thinking about how things had changed. The Black community tried to claim all my friend's after-session time, inviting her to "caucus" meetings and social gatherings. It did not occur to them that we might want to spend some time together while we were there. It was a bizarre and unsettling experience, for me in particular.

The strangest reaction of all came from her own cousin, who had lived in Atlanta for about twenty years and had not made one close White friend. When she entered our hotel room and discovered that her cousin's roommate was a White woman, she completely lost her bearings. It took her about twenty-four hours to deal with the fact that we were actually friends, and after that, we all had a good time together. (She has since moved to Seattle where she finds the atmosphere totally different and is very happy she made the move.) That experience was a reminder to me that it is not that long since slavery was a reality in that part of America; it takes many generations to change both conscious and unconscious ways of thinking.

Black communities in North America are not the only ones to experience racism. In preparation for a speaker who was coming to one of our programs to talk about racism in our society, we had invited any student who regarded themselves as part of a visible minority to participate in a discussion prior to his visit so that they could articulate what they wanted to say and to ask our guest. From our perspective, my Black colleague's and mine, all but two of the participants in the group fit that category. Another two learners were a somewhat ambiguous call due to their mixed racial background. We were surprised to find only four women who easily claimed their non-White ancestry. Women of Asian and Native (Latin American Native) ancestry in the program did not see themselves as part of a visible minority. When my colleague worked with the group and discussed race from a perspective of pride, they changed their minds and decided to own their ancestry with pride. Until then, many of the learners had done whatever they could to deny it, even to themselves.

Those of us who are not immediately affected by racism tend not to be aware of its very painful consequences. Those victimized by racism may or may not discuss it with their own families or members of their own communities. They, however, have often learned that it is not safe to discuss racism with White people, who have been, in their experience, all too quick to accuse them of having a chip on their shoulder, or whose obvious discomfort with the topic does not encourage them to take that risk in similar situations in future. Others affected by racism may not be prepared themselves to name it for what it is, and prefer to deny its existence, or admit that it happens to other people but not to them.

I cannot think of many things more psychologically scarring than to be repeatedly victimized for no other reason than the colour of one's skin or the shape of one's nose. Learners bear many scars when they come into our classrooms. Those scars which result from war and poverty, they can wear somewhat openly, knowing that we will, if not understand, at least accept. But those wounds which result from racism, they may feel they need to hide from us because we would not, could not, understand. In addition to trying to understand the issues better, both in terms of our own learned racism and the presence of it in our communities, we can also let learners know that we are aware of these issues and that it is okay to talk about them openly. The learners need to know what their human rights are and how they can be exercised in a helpful manner, both for their own benefit and for the benefit of those who will follow them. (Chapter 10 discusses race and ethnicity in our classrooms.)

Degree of Traumatization

Refugees in particular often come into ESL classrooms with experiences as foreign to their teachers as the new country is to them. Their psyches and emotions may be raw, and they may react in ways that those around them find inexplicable and unacceptable. As educators, we cannot afford either to be overwhelmed, frightened, or awash in sympathy when such incidents occur. Such learners need to be supported in ways which give them the space to heal themselves and the strength to do so. One common error that educators make, with good intentions, is to solicit their stories of horror. Boat people were asked outright if they were raped on the boats, political refugees were asked if they had had to kill anyone. In short, people's privacy was invaded. People who are traumatized often have difficulty discussing these experiences, even with those to whom they are close, much less with someone who has power over them such as a teacher.

Our role in this situation, I suggest, is to support such learners in learning as they are able and not to push them. We can refer these students to community resources if they exist and when the learner expresses the readiness for such assistance. Most of us have no idea what such individuals need, and we can make the situation worse by intervening where we have neither understanding nor skill. We can be loving and caring, but we must keep an appropriate distance to allow people in pain to do what they need to do. If they want our help or our friendship, they will seek that out in their own time. In the meantime, let us be present to their being without being intrusive or thinking we can or should rescue anyone.

Religious Beliefs

Some people come to their new country with no religious beliefs, while others come with strongly set beliefs and religions about which we may know little or nothing. How can we accommodate these individuals in ways that respect their beliefs, while at the same time preparing them for what to expect, both in the labour market and in the community?

Christmas is a time of year that brings out these questions. I am one of many teachers who has taught Christmas carols at Christmas time, thinking it was a fun way to give some cultural capital to learners who would be hearing these songs everywhere during the season. I have not taught Christmas carols for several years, not since a staff member pointed out how insensitive this practice was to non-Christian learners. She suggested that instead of a Christmas party, we have a celebration of all faiths, where all the learners who wanted to participate could do some sort of ceremony that would introduce us to their religion and their celebrations.

This we did and how beautiful it was. The Moslems chanted prayers for us with prayer rugs and shawls. The Buddhists chanted their prayers while burning incense and bowing in honour to Buddha on an altar they had prepared. Some learners showed us dances and songs that belonged to their faiths. And, of course, the Christians sang carols in many languages and brought a Christmas tree to the gathering. This was one of the most memorable Christmases I have had. Learners who did not excel in learning English arose as leaders when it came to planning and delivering these presentations. We saw many of the students in a whole new light, as did their classmates. The dignity which ensued for those learners stayed with them for weeks to come, as they stood tall in their classrooms.

To be sensitive to our learners' religious beliefs, we can recognize the feast days and special holidays of learners by allowing them to be absent or leave early on these days, and by respecting that the celebrants of Ramadan (an Islamic celebration involving a month of fasting from sundown to sunset) may not be as energetic during that time as they are otherwise. This does not mean we would lead people to expect that they will be able to take time off work in future for these occasions, but it does mean that in some situations it would be okay to ask. If the employer says no, they either have to accept that or to seek employment with a more flexible employer.

We also have to find ways to deal with reality in the labour market. In most communities, wearing a hijab (a headdress often worn by Muslim women), will make it more difficult for a woman to find a good job. In some cases, this garment could be regarded as a safety hazard, if for example, it were worn around high-speed equipment where the fabric could get caught and cause an accident. In other cases, it is a matter of people fearing what they do not understand. While it should not matter if a Punjabi woman wears her ethnic costume or Western fashion, it may interfere in her finding work or even accommodation. It is up to us to present this information to learners—about how Canadians may judge these cultural customs, and let them make their own decisions as to what to do with it. It is a delicate road for us to walk because we do not want to be interpreted as condoning how others might discriminate against them for those practices.

History

I have often experienced myself as abysmally ignorant about the histories of many of the students I have taught, and this is a handicap. Even though I read the paper regularly and am always interested in reading about situations that pertain to learners, I often lack understanding of the historical information that would greatly enhance my under-standing, not only of the individuals I teach but also of the ways in which they interact with one another.

An example would be the Bosnian learners who came to many of our classrooms in 1998, and the Kosovars who came in 1999. Both groups of learners have come through horrific experiences. The inter-ethnic conflict in their own communities has been painful and difficult. The last thing they need to confront in their new country is the fact that here most people will not distinguish between Serbs, Croats, Bosnians, or Kosovars. For most Westerners, they are simply Yugoslavian. Some learners find it difficult to be in class with someone who, only weeks earlier, may have been shooting at them or a close relative. It will take a long time to heal these wounds, inner and outer, and we need not exacerbate them by being insensitive. If it is not possible to put these learners in different classes, at the very least, let us not ask these learn-ers to work in pairs when they feel antagonistic towards one another.

Another example might be in understanding why Ethiopians may feel so strongly against the separation of Eritrea. While the Eritrean cause has been popularized by the media in Western countries, this is a very controversial issue for nationalist Ethiopians who see the situation as similar to that of Quebec and the rest of Canada. A friend of mine of

Eritrean parentage was raised in Addis Abeba. She gets very impatient with the readiness of Canadians to support the Eritrean cause, which she feels has been taken up by Americans with self-serving interests, not in keeping with the best interests of either Ethiopia or Eritrea. There is indeed much evidence to suggest that Africa, far from being in charge of its own destiny, is still very much at the hands of more powerful nations who use the African nations as pawns in their own political chess game.

The danger in reading history lies in forgetting that it is always written from one particular perspective. There are almost always many opposing perspectives about how history can be written. (Have you noticed that when the "Indians" of our own history won a battle against the White soldiers, it was called a massacre, but when the soldiers won, it was called a great victory?) It is hard to know what to believe, and the only way to sort through it all is to acquire as many perspectives as we possibly can, and do our best to make sense of them. In spite of the challenges of understanding complex issues, we need at the very minimum to be aware of the issues and not to take sides which would serve only to alienate some of the learners we teach. In addition, I have learned to steer clear of learning about such issues during class time because it can lead to painful conflict and unhappiness among learners.

Age

I have had the great privilege of working with several seniors' groups over the last ten years. I say privilege because, for all the challenges of working with their health and memory loss issues (in some), there is something very special about working with multicultural seniors groups. These learners accept the fact of their own demise and are cherishing each day and each learning opportunity as an occasion to celebrate. We did a research project with federal government funding some years back, and one of the questions we wanted to ask was whether or not seniors learned better in mixed-gender classes or women-only classes. (Under the terms of our funding we were not allowed to have men's classes.) We also wondered if it made any difference to their learning which type of class they were in.

In the interviews that followed the classes, women who had been in the women-only classes tended to support that class composition, although they were not adamant about it. Women in the mixed classes almost always said it didn't matter. "At this age, same-same," they would say. In the seniors' classes, I found that the things that tended often to divide younger learners—education, job experience, social status, and gender—were not barriers for seniors. They had lived life, were prepared for death, and simply enjoyed new experiences as they came. It was really refreshing to work with them. In a way, that surprised me because my experience of elders in my own society has been the opposite. The seniors I've known have often been very set in their ways and have been unwilling to tolerate things that were outside their experience. Not so with these immigrant seniors.

From a purely physical standpoint, seniors do not have the facility of movement or endurance that younger learners have, nor do many have the same ability to remember new information. Their priorities for learning are different. Age is one of the many factors we have to take into account in planning programs for learners, the Subjects of our classrooms.

Workshop Activity I

Go back to your years as a learner. Which teachers did you like best? What was it about them that made you enjoy their classes most? How did you feel about yourself in their presence? How did you feel about others in their presence? How did you feel about learning in their presence? Have this discussion with friends. You may find it quite revealing.

CHAPTER 3

Principles in the ESL Classroom

Questions to reflect upon:

- By reflecting on your own practice as a teacher, can you identify any principles that you feel empower participants in their lives?
- Are you conscious of particular values with which you choose to guide your own life?
- In what ways might you offer those values to learners without imposing them?
- In what ways do you let learners know you respect their freedom of choice, when their values are not consistent with your own?

Identifying Working Principles for the Classroom

Most of us could probably identify some principles we hold that influence our work in the classroom. I suspect, however, that we see those principles as being personal and private, having little or nothing to do with the curriculum. I suggest that the identification of a set of working principles can be a gift to the learners and to ourselves.

A *principle* is a fundamental truth or law that serves as the basis of reasoning or action. Those principles of which we have a sense of ownership lead to a personal or shared code of conduct. In the techno-logical worldview, which dominates our thinking as a society, we seldom think about the values we hold, or the principles from which we act. If someone were to ask us our philosophy, most of us would be hard pressed to give much of an answer.

A *working principle* is one we have chosen to *apply* in a particular context or for a particular reason with the intent of making our lives better for ourselves and for those around us. When we call something a working principle, we are not concerned with a universal definition but only with a definition that suits our purposes.

Participation, Commitment, and Community

My awareness of the value of concretely stated principles in the class-room, began in the early eighties while I was doing a project with some women in a housing development in the east end of Edmonton. (See *From One Educator to Another: A Window on Participatory Education*, Virginia Sauvé.) Most of the participants in the program were women with limited education who survived their day to day challenges of life on social assistance. As we worked with the women, my attention was drawn to three notions which were significant in the extent to which each participant derived value from the program: *participation*, *commitment*, and *community*.

Those participants who came regularly, asked lots of questions, expressed their ideas, told their stories, and generally immersed themselves in what we were doing seemed to be learning a lot and enjoying the experience. Those women who made a decision to change something in their lives and followed through on it, in spite of their fears, were able to overcome their barriers. Those participants who were willing to share with the community, to reach out and support others in the group, seemed to value the presence of the group the most in their community.

As I observed these things, I felt it would be useful to talk about my observations with the group and see what they thought. I did so and, to my surprise, they took them as obvious. They did not have the words—participation, commitment, and community—but they certainly accepted the ideas. By putting words to our experiences, we could be more conscious in understanding our decisions and in discussing our inner struggles with one another. We put these words up on a poster on the wall where they served to remind us of their value in moving forward in our lives.

Other Working Principles

When I returned to my work with immigrant women in job training programs, I thought to myself that these ideas might be useful, so I hung the poster again. As I worked in the new programs, new principles emerged—new ideas which had value in our working together: *acknowledgement, compassion, risk, truth, action/reflection (praxis).*[1] These words, too, found their way on to the poster, and I invited learners to add their own as we became conscious of them.

---

1 The Greek had three words for "practise," praxis being the highest form of practise. It represents the dialectical union of action and reflection.

We began to understand how these ideas overlapped and complemented one another. We saw that when we are generous in our acknowledgement of others, we build community. When we take the risks of exposing ourselves and telling the truth, there can be authenticity in our community. When we reflect and act, we are living out our commitments to ourselves and to others. When we show compassion to the one who is hurting, we are not only supporting them, but we are creating the kind of environment we ourselves would like to have when we are hurting.

Accountability

In a workshop I attended as a participant, I discovered the amazing power of the notion of *accountability,* and it made a profound difference to my sense of power over my own experience. To think that a mere idea could hold such transcendent power to change our lives— still surprises me. Accountability, in the sense that I mean it, is not the dictionary understanding of the term, which is indistinguishable from responsibility—a notion that others hold us to. Rather, it is a choice one makes to *account* for one's own experience without resorting to blame. When one chooses accountability, one is not interested in whose fault something is. Rather, one is interested in what it means to the one whose experience it is, and in what power that individual can take in that situation to make things better for himself/herself, and those he/she cares about. Accountability is accounting for one's one experience in a way that takes power over it.

In the act of blaming a person for something, we are, in some sense, giving away our power to do something about that which we do not like. This is not the same as saying that others are not responsible for what they do. However, when we get stuck in blame, we do not see what power we have to change things for ourselves. Accountability, the alternative, is therefore a very empowering notion. It is not an easy, comfortable notion. Far from it. It is difficult. From childhood on, most of us have been conditioned to look for someone or something to blame for our troubles; thereby avoiding any unpleasant consequences of feeling guilty or responsibility for changing things. Blame enables us to feel self-righteous, but it can also leave us dependent on others to change our circumstances. In blame, we often see ourselves as a victim and the other as a perpetrator. That gives the perpetrator the power over us if we get stuck there. In terms of finding solutions to life's problems, blame is often largely irrelevant. In accountability, we put our energy into recognizing what we can and cannot do in a situation, and we opt to do that which we can.

Response-Ability

We can choose accountability as individuals or as a group. Either way, we are choosing to push our parameters of power in any given situation and make the kind of choices that enable us to have greater control over our lives in the future. In addition, we can redefine the word "responsibility" by going back to its roots and looking at what it means to be *response-able*. If accountability is choosing to take care of ourselves, *response-ability*, as a working principle, is choosing, out of our abundance, to respond to others in their places of need. Whether it be material, emotional, or another need, we can, if we are reasonably stable ourselves, choose to respond to that other in a way that makes life better for him or her.

These two notions, accountability and response-ability, have been very valuable, both in my life and in my work as an educator in recent years. These concepts are of greatest value, perhaps, to learners with little literacy—people who have not learned to live in a world of word-symbols and concepts the way readers have. Many literacy learners know, however, what it is to want power and lack it; any notion by which such learners can extend their sense of power over their own lives is readily understood and embraced.

Justice and Self-Care

In addition to the aforementioned principles, various groups I've worked with have added other principles, as needed. It is very important for some learners to add the principle of *justice*, as problematic as that can be if people seeking justice go beyond fairness and equality towards judgment and vindication, values which are inconsistent with the other principles named.

Another principle I added when I began to work with housekeepers in our six-city hospitals was *self-care*. I found that these hard-working men and women were so busy taking care of other people and trying to please others that they were injuring themselves. Normally, accountability would cover this area, but in this case, we needed a principle to draw health, well-being, and safety to their attention in a clear way.

What do we do with principles in an ESL classroom?

What do these principles have to do with teaching English as a Second Language? For one thing, they are words and we are in the business of teaching words. It is always a matter of judgment to decide which words to teach and which words to let learners discover for themselves. Because it is easier to teach concrete words rather than abstract ones, we tend to first teach those practical words that people need to do their basic functional tasks in daily life: buy groceries, pay rent, find a job, ask for directions, and be friendly with others. If we were teaching English as a *Foreign* Language, these words might be enough. But if we are teaching English as a *Second* Language, and if we are teaching immigrants who plan to make their home in this new country, we are teaching also about settlement and integration. If we then decide that we want to educate for freedom, for self-sufficiency, for empowerment, we need to teach in ways and with words which will make that possible. Is it appropriate in every context? No, of course not. But it is appropriate in many.

Teaching with Working Principles

It is inappropriate to impose values on a learner, and principles certainly embody values. The easiest way to teach these principles is not by designing a lesson to teach them, but rather by introducing the words one by one as situations present themselves, and by naming the realities we see in the relationships of the classroom. By introducing a word to name something the group has already experienced is to ensure that the learners already understand the experience; they lack only the English word, and, in a few cases, the semantic notion to describe it.

If we have listened to someone stewing about a problem she is having and feeling totally helpless about, that may be the time to introduce the notions of *blame* and *accountability*. For example, we can be very angry at a landlord who unscrupulously takes advantage of the naiveté of an immigrant by charging her for placing garbage bags in the back lane each week. We can indeed blame the landlord for all the money that the unfortunate woman has lost due to his dishonesty. But blaming does not change her situation. We can play rescuer and call the landlord ourselves and threaten to expose him to the police if he continues his evil practice. That may stop him; it may not. Or, we can ensure that this woman knows her rights and how to stand up for them. This was a real situation. The class discussed her problem, and the woman went back to her landlord and told him in no uncertain terms that she knew her rights and would not be paying him any more money. After that, he left her alone. Resolving this situation herself empowered the learner far more than if one of the staff had solved her problem for her. Her actions gave her confidence that she was capable of standing up for herself—and she let the landlord know that she would no longer be duped.

For a more positive example of naming our experience, I turn to a story that took place many years ago, when I was teaching an ESL class composed of Latin Americans, Vietnamese, and two Turkish-Cypriots. (If you have read the other book of this series, forgive me. This story was included in it.) This is one of my favourite stories because for me it captures the heart of what ESL is about. I had inherited this class from a teacher who was well loved by her students. They did not want a new teacher and were quite sad about the switch. I, in turn, could see some conflicts between the cultural groups within the class, as well as the isolation of the two Turkish-Cypriots, who happened to be mother and son.

Because this group had experienced no common ground with one another, I knew we needed to create some, so I suggested a winter barbecue. It was late February, and while there was still a lot of snow on the ground, it was not bitterly cold. I asked them if they were interested in a barbecue; they said they were, and I left them to plan it. I was beginning to doubt whether we would ever be able to get back to our curriculum as they argued about everything. One group wanted to do a potluck, and another group wanted to buy the food and make everyone pay for it. The mother and son wanted nothing to do with either plan because they did not trust anyone else to ensure that there was no pork in the food. They said they would bring their own food. Finally, they reached an agreement and the day arrived. We had our barbecue and everyone seemed to be having a good time. After eating, we decided to go for a walk.

During our walk, we approached the top of a steep hill covered with ice. Before I could ponder how we were all going to get to the bottom, an elderly Chinese man in the class winked and leaped into the air. He landed on his rear end upon which he proceeded down the hill, laughing as he went. Most of the class followed until there remained only two older women and myself. The older woman's son and husband started walking up the hill to help them down. But these two women would have none of it. They linked arms, a nearly blind Chilean woman and the Turkish-Cypriot woman, and they too slid down the hill, arms and legs akimbo, black stockings windmilling with their descent. I joyfully followed. And everyone sat at the bottom of the hill, ice melting beneath us, as we laughed and laughed and laughed. The laughter was more than the moment. It was a release of a lot of energy, fear, and pain. We could not stop laughing for a long time, and when finally we did, there was total silence. No one wanted to lose the joy of that moment. Finally, the old Turkish-Cypriot woman struggled to her feet, came over and hugged me, and said, "Teacher, good. First time in Canada laugh." Those were her first English words in my presence, and they said so very much. I wonder what might have happened had the Chinese man not had the wisdom he did to make the first move?

In that brief afternoon, this group had created the necessary bridges of community among themselves and with me. We had shared a very special moment together. I will not say there were never any conflicts after that, but I can truthfully say that the relationships within that classroom had changed. When conflicts did arise after that, people could discuss them openly and resolve them. And I no longer felt like an outcast. If that event were to happen today, I would name the feelings we felt as *community* and explore it with them. I might look for other words to talk about why we had laughed so long and hard, and what difference it had made for us to have had that experience together. I would look for other opportunities to discuss the experience of community in their lives and in our shared society.

Creating a Principles Poster

I have mentioned using a poster to remind us of the principles we have named. I suggest that when you first find a principle that the members of the group can agree on as valuable, you begin your poster there, and add new principles as they arise. After you have named several principles, you may wish to review them by designing a problem-solving exercise in which several scenarios are outlined, each needing one or more of the principles to be applied for their resolution. People can work on these scenarios in groups and usually enjoy doing so. You can also encourage people to share stories about applying these principles outside the classroom. We learn vicariously from one another, and participants place more value on these notions when they hear their classmates' stories, and they see how someone has consciously used an idea and found it effective.

Sample Scenarios from a Workplace Curriculum

The following mini-scenarios are taken from an exercise designed to review a set of principles that a group of housekeepers from six hospitals have been working with. In the exercise, the housekeepers are asked which of the principles would be most effective in applying to the resolution of the problem presented. (Following each scenario is a short discussion, not part of the exercise, to provide you with some context for understanding the importance of these scenarios to these workers.)

I._____ Management announces that housekeeping will be privatized within one year's time, and the union asks housekeepers to vote in favour of a strike.

The housekeepers are very fearful of the possibility of privatization. Workers who come from countries where the labour movements have been strong will instantly understand that they have to stand up for their rights. Those workers who come from countries that have been highly dictatorial in their politics may have a hard time knowing what to do. Accustomed to living in fear, they have no experience in achieving success by standing together as a group.

If their jobs are privatized, all of these workers will have the following choice: they can seek work with private companies for approximately one-third of the wages they are getting now, but with no benefits or seniority, or they can seek other work after doing this job for as long as thirty years. Because some workers are ready to retire anyway, they may not see the importance of sticking together in this fight for the recognition of their skills and commitment, they have brought to their jobs in the interests of the patients.

The answer to this scenario is *community*. Unions are only effective when workers stand together. There is great power in community.

2. _____ There is a meeting at your workplace. You have something you want to say, but you are nervous that someone might laugh at you or argue with you, and thereby embarrass you. On the other hand, if you say nothing, your problem will remain the same.

Different cultures have different ways of understanding the roles of different persons within their culture. In some, women do not speak. In others, the poor do not speak up to the rich. In some, the employee does not speak up to the employer. In addition, those who speak English as a second language are often self-conscious about their English and find that other immigrants are the most critical of all—talking about them behind their backs.

In this scenario, it seems easier to many learners to say nothing at all. Teaching acceptable forms of participation, however, is part of teaching empowerment in this culture. In the particular project where this exercise is used with successive groups of workers, one of the early observations of management following the program was, and I quote, "I used to have trouble getting them to say anything at the meetings. Now, I can't shut them up." (He was very happy with the results.)

The sought-after answer is *participation*.

3. _____ A nurse is about to cross your newly waxed floor, and a doctor stops her and says, "How about walking over here?"

Housekeepers have a lot of anger and sadness over their sense of not being valued in the hospitals. Some workers have enough self-confidence to say something when someone does something thoughtless, but most workers either think it will not do any good, or fear the consequences of speaking out. When another person intervenes on their behalf, it is important to acknowledge that person with some expression of appreciation for what they have done.

The sought-after answer is *acknowledgement.*

4. _____ You hurt your back while doing some gardening at home on the weekend. You were asked at work to help move some heavy armchairs from a storage area into the lounge. Normally, you would not mind, but today you are a little worried about your back.

Until recent cuts to health care, getting a job in a hospital was tantamount to having your career in place until you retired. (Many older workers find it hard to believe that twenty years of service means nothing more than a severance package, if their companies are privatized.) Because previously the employees perceived that the hospital was committed to them, they responded with a strong sense of commitment to their work. This results in, among other things, their doing what they are asked to do, even when it is not part of their job description. In this case, moving chairs is part of the Attendent 2's job, who are men. The Attendent 1's, or housekeepers, do not, at least in theory, do heavy work. There are many examples of workers injuring themselves when they are trying to be helpful and co-operative. In some cases, they do not know how to care for themselves while doing heavy work because this has not been part of their training. In other cases, they are already injured and simply cannot handle the heavy work.

The desired answer here is *self-care.*

Workshop Activity 1

Imagine that you are teaching a class of male and female immigrant seniors. Most are reasonably well-educated, and between the ages of 60 and 84. Most are living with an adult child and his or her family. Some take care of their grandchildren. Some live alone or with their spouses. You have worked with the group for about ten months and the following principles have emerged as significant to this group: hope, faith, cooperation, truth, persistence, acknowledgment, and fairness. Make up a review exercise, such as the one above, using scenarios that are relevant to the lives of the seniors. The idea is to identify one or more principles for each scenario; this practise empowers the individual to deal with each situation in a positive way. Here is one sample to get you going:

_____ Mrs. Lee lives with her son and his wife and two children. Both the parents work. The older child is in Grade 2 and the youngest is in kindergarden. She sees the children off to school in the morning and has to be there when the little one gets home at 12:30, and when the older one gets home at 4:00. She usually cooks dinner for the family, who have sponsored her to come to this country.

Mrs. Lee's problem is that she has no money of her own, and when she asks for money, even to buy the special soap she needs for her skin, her daughter-in-law complains and gets angry with her. She has no money to buy birthday gifts for her grandchildren or stamps to send letters to her friends in Taiwan. Nor can she afford to go on a fieldtrip to the botanical gardens with her classmates. She is very poor, and she feels totally dependent on her son and his wife but very upset with how they treat her.

One would not use this scenario in Mrs. Lee's class for that would humiliate her. But seniors need to be aware of the problem of elder abuse in all its forms, and this kind of neglect or lack of respect for this woman's labour and her basic needs is surely abusive. A scenario like this will generate a lot of discussion around the needs of grandparents living with their children and the problems of cross-cultural conflict. At the root of this situation, and the reason it is all the more painful for Mrs. Lee, is that she knows in her country her son and daughter-in-law would not behave in this way. For one thing, the daughter-in-law would have stayed home with her children, and for another, elders are always treated with great respect. Mrs. Lee feels like she made a terrible mistake in leaving her friends and family to come and help out her son, and if she had the money, she would go home. As it is, she is too embarrassed for her son, to tell people at home about her problem and ask them for money.

Several of the principles apply here. There is the basic principle of fairness that is being violated. There is the need to remain hopeful and have faith that the situation can be corrected. There is the need for truth. This woman needs to be truthful with her son, and if that is not helpful, with someone who can help her to remove herself from this situation if need be. In any case, there is no "right" answer to this question. Rather, the group will use the scenario to explore issues that they might find too threatening to enter into in regards to their own situations but which they can enter into in regards to the mythical Mrs. Lee.

If you have not worked with seniors, you may want to get some ideas from teachers who have, or from a group of learners before doing the exercise.

Workshop Activity 2

The story of the winter barbecue has been, for me, one of those "signature moments" that stays clearly in my mind as embodying a significant learning in my career as an educator. Can you recall one or more "signature moments" in your teaching that have become markers or truth-holders in your understanding of what is important in what we do? Again, this activity is most valuable if shared with a group.

CHAPTER 4

Values and Ethics: Towards a Code of Conduct

Questions to reflect upon:

- What kind of regrets have you had in relation to something you did or did not do regarding a student or students?
- Have you witnessed other teachers behaving in ways that you felt were unethical—but you felt powerless or unwilling to do anything about it?
- Do the organizations for which you have worked have policies that incorporate elements of a code of ethics regulating unacceptable behaviour on the part of a teacher? If not, how do you account for that?
- Have you identified behaviours that you would consider to be outside your comfort zone in your relationships with students or staff?

Problematic Scenarios

Picture these scenarios and take note of your own reactions to them:

1. A teacher invites her students to her church for a New Year's Eve social gathering with her fellow parishioners.

2. A teacher dates her adult student, inobtrusively of course.

3. A teacher, unhappy with the administration of the school where he works, spends several minutes of every class complaining to the students about his boss, about the policies of the school, and about how ridiculous all the rules are. He spends other class time telling his students about his many problems with his health, his marriage, and his house.

4. A women's class has students from seven different countries. The teacher opens every afternoon class with a fifteen-minute circle massage where each person massages the neck of the person in front of her.

5. A teacher who is keen on ecology teaches her level two students all about Blue Boxes for recyling, using menstrual cups instead of sanitary napkins, and buying earth-friendly products. She spends about two weeks on this unit in a fifteen-week course.

6. A school that finds itself short of students offers current students $50 a head for any referrals who register in an ESL program, and $100 a head for any EFL students who register in an international program. All ESL students in the school are there on government tuition and monthly support.

7. A teacher is experienced by her adult students as exceedingly authoritarian and not open to suggestions or criticism. What the teacher decides is law. Period.

8. An ESL teacher, newly-divorced, finds herself spending a lot of time visiting a couple of students in their homes. She has meals with them, gets to know their children and spouses, and helps them with problems they are experiencing in adapting to life in their new country.

9. A teacher accepts with thanks the gift of a raincoat from a student who has just joined her class. Two months later, that teacher's immediate supervisor accepts a lovely ring with rubies and a diamond from a student whose husband is a goldsmith. The supervisor has assisted in an appeal to increase the learner's allowance from the government agency paying her monthly stipend.

10. Several teachers and a junior administrator become aware that a colleague is undermining his employer with all sorts of fallacious gossip. As well, there are many indications that this teacher may be using his position to exploit young men, at least emotionally and probably sexually. His colleagues and supervisor do nothing.

As you read the above ten scenarios, you will probably find yourself reacting strongly to some and finding them unacceptable. However, you may look at others and say, "Yeah, so what's wrong with that?" To enter into our discussion of ethics in ESL classrooms, I would like to explore each of these scenarios, and to provide some information and thoughts on each that may not have been apparent to you when you read them initially. While I have chosen these scenarios because I personally judge the situations to be problematic, I can also understand that some of you will disagree, and may, in fact, want strongly to defend the teacher's decision. These are all real scenarios. My purpose in offering them is not to judge the teachers, but rather to open up some much-needed discussion on how our profession, our host organizations, and ourselves need to develop some clearly defined ethics in relation to the work we do.

A. A teacher invites her students to her church for a New Year's Eve social gathering with her fellow parishioners.

This teacher is a wonderful human being who has devoted herself totally to the service of her students. She is also a dedicated Christian of an evangelical persuasion. She believes strongly in being friends with her students and went out of her way to organize this event with her church, seeing this gathering as a way to provide one-on-one communication opportunities for her students and introduce them to valuable contacts which could help them in their job search or solve other problems they were experiencing.

Her administrator found out about the invitation after it had already happened when a student came to complain. The administrator went to talk to the teacher. The teacher said she had not pressured the students to attend the event, and they were free to say no. Although logically the administrator could understand all the arguments the teacher was making to support her action, the administrator felt that the invitation was wrong. She instructed the teacher to cease such social offers and to ask permission for any such group extra-curricular activities in future.

In the meantime, the administrator decided to do some research. She talked to colleagues in the settlement field, and they strongly supported her position. She talked to immigrant friends of long standing, and they too supported her position. Her friends told her stories of how they had encountered similar pressure from their sponsors to attend their churches, and how they felt obligated to do so because the sponsors had helped them so much. But they also felt uncomfortable, for they were Buddhists. The Islamic people in the class said no to the invitations but felt angry that they had been asked.

I do not question the teacher's stated intentions here. It is possible that she honestly saw the church members as adding to the students' learning opportunities and feelings of belonging. However, she is naive if she thinks that the students can feel genuinely free to say no, or if she thinks that these events will not change the learners' experience in the classroom.

First, there is the issue of power. A teacher has an enormous amount of power over the lives of her students. She can encourage them or embarrass them, declare them successful, or in some cases fail them, and she can make their lives pleasant or unbearable in the hours they are in class. For that reason, most students see it as being in their interest to do what the teacher wants, regardless of what they want. Secondly, those students who participate in such events are actually changing their relationship with the teacher and with the students. Teachers usually become closer to those students they spend time with, laugh with, and talk to. This results in those students who do *not* participate in these events feeling they do not have the background to participate in discussions which happen when they *are* in class. They begin to feel left out and to resent their new status in the class. They also attribute aspects of the teacher's friendly behaviour, rightly or wrongly, as a demonstration of favouritism towards those students who have participated in her agenda.

When I began to teach in a large government institution some years ago, I was told never to discuss religion or politics in the classroom. I had trouble with that directive because it seemed dishonest to me. The issue, I believed, was not in *what* to discuss but rather in *how* to discuss it. If I discuss an issue with an intent to persuade someone else of my views, then I am taking unfair advantage of my status as teacher and imposing my views on the other. If, on the other hand, I am willing to listen without passing judgment on the person or people speaking, without changing my treatment of them because of what they shared, and without expecting that they will agree with me, I see no harm in expressing myself and encouraging others to do likewise. Many would disagree with me. And to be sure, I have not escaped problems because of this view. I also have to be very careful not to let the excessive zealousness of a few dominate the interests of the many. But this is for each teacher to decide.

B. A teacher dates an adult student, unobtrusively of course.

Many institutions would have hard and fast rules governing appropriate teacher-student relationships. This example is not given for those institutions that already have such policies, but is intended rather for the many programs throughout the country not thus governed.

As adults, we tend to form friendships and sexual relationships with the people we are attracted to in our lives. As teachers, we spend a lot of our time with adult immigrant learners and, for sure, we are going to be attracted to some of them more than others. I have known many ESL and EFL teachers who have married men and women who initially were their students. I see nothing wrong with that.

However, dating a *current* student can present problems. For one thing, it changes your relationship with that student in the class, no matter how careful you are to ensure that this is not the case. Students may notice this or not. Whether or not the students are aware of what is going on, unequal relationships are created within the classroom, and for that reason alone, this situation should be avoided. It is even worse if the student sees his or her relationship with the teacher as a gain in his or her own power and brags about it to other students in the program. If a learner boasts about his or her relationship, the teacher's reputation may well be ruined, and potentially the program's reputation will be damaged as well.

My suggestion to the teacher who is drawn to one of his or her students is to hang on to that attraction until the person graduates from your program. Everyone will be spared a lot of grief, and if the attraction is real, it can wait.

C. *A teacher who feels unhappy with the administration of the school where he works spends a good deal of time in every class complaining to the students about his boss, about the policies of the school, and about how ridiculous all the rules are. He frequently tells his students about his many problems with his health, his marriage, and his house.*

I need not spend much time explaining this scenario. I think most readers understand how inappropriate the man's behaviour was. He was using his students, and in doing so, was placing them in a very uncomfortable position. On one hand, some students dreaded coming to school. They had enough problems in their own lives without spending valuable time listening to his. (One woman confided that she had developed terrible stomachaches every morning at the thought of coming to class. When the teacher was asked to leave and she had another teacher, her stomachaches disappeared.) The students felt obliged to offer him their sympathy, even though they were angry with his unprofessional conduct. They were feeling that he was expecting them to take care of him, and this was not a time in their lives when they felt they could or should do that. On the other hand, the learners went some time without reporting his behaviour because they did not want to feel responsible for getting their teacher into trouble.

Being a professional means putting the learners' interests ahead of our own needs. A teacher who is unable to do that should not be in the classroom. This man needed help but was unable to see that. His leave-taking was very unpleasant. He threatened the director's life and blamed her for all his problems.

We must also question the decisions of those teachers who knew of his behaviour but took no action to stop it. It may have been easier to not get involved, but was it right? I think not.

D. *A women's class has students from seven different countries. The teacher opens every afternoon class with a fifteen-minute circle massage where each person massages the neck of each person in front of her.*

This very caring teacher wanted all her students to be friends. She recognized that stress was a fact of the students' lives, and she saw massage as something practical she could do to provide relief. Some of the students thought the massage was great, and other learners found it bizarre and uncomfortable, but felt like they had no choice but to participate and act like they enjoyed it. Like the teacher who took her students to socials at her church, this teacher fully believed that she was doing something valuable for her students. But, she failed to recognize the cultural aspects of this action and the consequences of the power imbalance between herself and the students.

This teacher was herself from another country. She spoke her own language to those students of the same language group, who found it easier to understand concepts she was trying to explain in class. These same students, I suspect, may not have been as comfortable with neck and shoulder massage in a classroom had another teacher introduced it, but because they already liked and identified with this teacher, they accepted it. Other students, however, already feeling excluded from the linguistic exchange they did not understand, were further alienated by their teacher's behaviour for which they had no context and which they did not attach to typical teacher behaviour. These learners were already in the minority, and giving neck massages became but one more activity from which they felt excluded. For them, protesting against something the majority seemed to enjoy was a non-viable option, regardless of how distasteful this practice was to them. (One student eventually confided in another teacher on staff, who spoke her language. She explained how she and the other students felt who did not speak the teacher's language.)

E. A teacher who is keen on ecology teaches her level two students all about Blue Boxes for recyling, using menstrual cups instead of sanitary napkins, and buying earth-friendly products. She spends about two weeks on this unit, in a fifteen-week course.

This teacher made an assumption, which is commonly made by some very excellent teachers, that a worthy agenda is equally worthy in all contexts; and therefore imposes a personal agenda on her class. Now as teachers, we all do that to some extent. It only becomes controversial when our personal agendas are sufficiently non-mainstream that they draw attention to our curriculum revisions. No one would deny that sound ecological practices are a worthy component in any curriculum over the long term. This teacher's choice is questionable because of who her students are, what level they are at in their language learning, and how much time they have to study in the program.

Our guiding principle in deciding which language to teach and which language to omit has to be based on the real priorities of the learners, and we learn these by facilitating student participation in the ongoing emergence of a curriculum. In this case, her students were refugee women, most of whom came from relatively non-industrialized countries. They had probably lived more in keeping with sound ecological principles than compared to us, not by choice so much as by circumstance.

Had this teacher merely introduced her students to Blue Box recycling and even to menstrual cups as a personal choice rather than a social norm, we would probably see no problem. The fact that she made up a whole unit on the environment, which took two weeks to "cover," is problematic. I personally do not see that studying environmental issues was the most effective use of time for that group of women at that time. Their major concern was finding employment.

F. *A school that finds itself short of students offers current students $50 a head for any referrals who register in an ESL program, and $100 a head for any EFL students who register in an international program. All ESL students are there on government tuition and monthly support.*

It is not only teachers who need a code of conduct but organizations as well. One school in our community used this strategy to recruit students. To cover the costs of paying the students, it would appear that the school increased the tuition which the government then pays on the student's behalf. To some, this may seem like a clever marketing idea. Personally, I find this practise reprehensible.

I first learned about this policy from a former student who had transferred to this school when we closed down our own school. She had come back to visit and said with some sadness that the new school was different from ours. All they think about, she said, was money, money, money. She said that now a lot of the students spent their free time trying to talk their friends into coming to this school instead of attending other schools throughout the city.

Obviously, this was an effective marketing ploy. But at what cost to the students? The students in these programs are very poor, or they would not qualify for government funding. The financial guidelines make life exceedingly difficult for the student whose expenses do not fit into their minimalist categories. If one's rent is higher than the guidelines, which is common, or if one sends money home to family, there is no way a learner has enough for his or her own needs as well as those of his or her immediate family. Such an offer is often irresistible to these students, and the school sees the learners' eagerness as yet another argument for doing it. How is a student to concentrate on learning when the focus is on making money? And of even greater concern is the effect this policy has on the student's relationships with others in his or her community. If the student's motive for recommending a school is personal financial gain rather than the best interest of the other learner, trust can be sadly broken between those individuals.

This school made a decision to put its own financial needs above the interests of the learners who study there.

G. *A teacher is experienced by her adult students as exceedingly authoritarian and not open to suggestions or criticism. What the teacher decides is law. Period.*

Most of us have witnessed this type of teacher. Such a teacher may have excellent knowledge of the language and of current language acquisition theory, and students accustomed to traditionally authoritative classrooms may respond very positively to such a teacher. However, for that teacher to be successful, he or she must have a very sound knowledge of what the learners need and are capable of, and must have students who accept this style of teaching. Otherwise, much is lost. Most critical, perhaps, is the sense of disrespect such a teacher conveys to her students in not being open to their suggestions or views. The person who has lost his or her bearings in a new country, language, and culture needs, above all, to maintain his or her personal dignity. When a learner is treated with disrespect by someone in authority, this can be the last straw that tumbles that individual into depression and despair. It is humiliating to learn a language. Language learners make errors that are very humorous to native speakers. It is also frustrating for learners when others do not understand what they are trying to say and when they do not understand what is being said to them. These emotions can leave them off-balance. I believe that it is of primary importance that the teachers of such learners show genuine respect for them, welcoming their input and ideas into the curriculum wherever feasible.

H. *An ESL teacher, newly divorced, finds herself spending a lot of time visiting a couple of students in their homes. She has meals with them, gets to know their children and spouses, and helps them with problems they are experiencing in adapting to life in their new country.*

Providing that such a teacher does not herself become a burden, getting together with a teacher outside the classroom can be a real blessing for the students whom she has favoured with her presence. Through these contacts students get opportunities to practise the language and learn about their new country. They feel like they have a friend. However, and it is a big however, what about the other students in the class?

This situation is not totally unlike the earlier one we explored where a teacher got romantically involved with a student. In both situations, the relationship of the teacher to the "chosen students" has been substantially altered by the closeness of their relationship outside the classroom. People who know one another well can often communicate without words. They anticipate one another's needs and wants. They read each other's body language. There is an ease to their interactions that anyone sensitive to body language can readily see. In addition, second language learners become very adept at reading body language since it cconveys meanings they do not understand in the spoken language. True or untrue, some learners may perceive that one student or group is enjoying favoured status, which of course they are, outside the classroom. This does not make for good relationships all-round *in* the classroom.

This close relationship between the teacher and some learners also creates problems if there is a problem with the "favoured" students. What is the teacher to do when her favourite student does something he or she should not do towards another student, or violates the policies of the school? Suddenly, things that should be straightforward become very complicated. If a teacher is prepared to serve all of her students extra-curricularly, then this is an option; but to socialize more with one student or small group of learners than with the others is problematic. Once again, it is better for the teacher to wait until an ESL program is concluded to take up that friendship.

I. A teacher accepts with thanks the gift of a raincoat from a student who has just joined her class. Two months later, that teacher's immediate supervisor accepts a lovely ring with rubies and a diamond from a student whose husband is a goldsmith. The supervisor assisted in an appeal to increase the learner's allowance from the government agency paying her monthly stipend.

Gift-giving is an area of great difficulty. When I first joined a large institution where I worked for many years, there was a policy forbidding any student from giving gifts to teachers. In the beginning, I saw no problem with this. The students were poor and needed their money for the necessities of life. The reality, however, was not so easy. Students were giving gifts to the teachers at the end of a class and hiding the fact. The teachers were accepting these presents because it felt very uncomfortable for them to do otherwise. In trying to convince students *not* to buy gifts, or, at the very least, to buy a small plant rather than an expensive gift, I frequently heard things like, "But we want you to have something you will remember us with, something that you will always have." They tended to buy vases, wall ornaments, and serving ware. Feeling the joy the learners got from giving a gift, I began to speak out against the no-gift policy, and it was changed providing that the students agreed to spend no more than ten dollars, and to give gifts only at the end of a class.

Nevertheless I am still uncomfortable with gift-giving because the moment you present such a policy there is the expectation that a gift is expected, and it should not be. In hindsight, I prefer the policy of a local settlement agency—any gifts given to one person are placed in the staff room for all to enjoy. Clients are told this up front, and the incentive to buy a gift for one individual is lost. However many students will bring food they have prepared for all to enjoy.

In spite of the obvious dilemmas around gift-giving, there are some instances which have been, in my perspective, clearly unethical. The raincoat was one such instance. I was walking down the corridor one day, when from an open classroom door, I saw this teacher put on a raincoat and model it for the class. She thanked the student who had given it to her and said how lovely it was. I was surprised since I knew this student had joined the program only one day earlier. I knew this teacher very well, and it was unthinkable for her to refuse a gift or to be other than very magnanimous in her expression of thanks. I was puzzled as to why the student would bring a gift to the teacher on her second day of class.

In discussing this situation, a colleague who had been an immigrant herself explained that for some students, giving a gift was a purchase of favours. She felt that this woman was assuring that when she needed help, it would be there for her. Sure enough, the next day a box was left in my mailbox—another raincoat with a neatly printed name on it. As it turned out, it was placed in my box by mistake; it was intended for the employment counselor who would be arranging the job placement for this woman. Both staff members felt they had to keep the coats so as not to insult the woman.

I disagree with that decision, but I understand their feelings. The staff as a whole was very uncomfortable with any policy that would bar gift-giving, for the same reasons that I had felt years earlier. The problem, however, is that when this type of gift-giving is allowed to occur, other students see that as a message—that giving gifts is necessary and does make a difference in the service they get from teachers and other staff.

The raincoat was a small problem compared to a gift given to another staff member whose job it was to assist students in their dealings with the funding agency. I had observed that this woman never brought lunch and yet always seemed to have plenty of food brought by the students. I naively thought that these gifts of food were just expressions of affection; until one day I saw firsthand how cleverly she appeared to recruit these contributions. (I am not sure if she did this deliberately or if she was quite unconscious as to the effects of her words and actions.) She was openly suggesting to the students that she really liked this food or that food, and that her children really liked it too. Many students then offered to cook a particular food for her the next day, and instead of refusing, she would thank them and smile. Some of the students told us later that they felt obligated to bring her food or other gifts in exchange for her help.

The most appaling gift, however, was a ruby and diamond ring, made for her by a goldsmith (a husband of one of the students). She showed her ring to several people with great pride, and the message was clear to the students. She knew that this family was very poor, and yet she saw no problem in accepting this gift. Nor could she see the negative consequences of letting people know she had received the gift. We need to ask ourselves when a gift is not a gift, but a purchase price for some service we are already paid to provide.

J. *Several teachers and a junior administrator become aware that a colleague is undermining his employer with all sorts of fallacious gossip. As well, there are many indications that this teacher may be using his position to exploit young men, at least emotionally and probably sexually. His colleagues and supervisor do nothing.*

While the teachers are uncomfortable with their observations of this colleague, none of them thinks it is their business to say anything. (Although when asked about the teacher's behaviour later, several members of the staff admit they knew.) They hear him ranting and raving—and close their doors. They see good-looking African men in their twenties come individually to meet him after class, and they feel very uncomfortable with this (especially when they hear the students talking about how often the teacher discusses sex in the classroom). Other staff overhear male and female learners alike discuss their discomfort over lunch, but the teachers do not want to get involved. After all, they reason, they have no proof. One teacher reports him to his immediate supervisor who talks to the teacher in question and, in turn, informs the manager of the situation, telling her that the problem seems to be solved. However, the supervisor does not check back to ensure that it is.

The supervisor in this instance is in a power struggle with her manager and finds it quite amusing that this teacher is critical of the manager. She sees it as in her interest not to take strong action. Meanwhile, the teacher who reported the teacher's behaviour feels like she has done what she needed to do, and her conscience is now clear.

At the end of the program, students come to the manager with numerous complaints about this teacher. They wonder why she did not know about these problems as they had talked directly with the supervisor and had assumed that she would tell the manager. While the manager knew about a few of the complaints, she had no idea of the extent of the problems.

At this point, the manager talked with the whole class and with the neighbouring teachers. She recognized that the teacher was very disturbed in his behaviour. She realized that the teachers knew the man had problems and had assumed that she did also. The manager saw that the supervisor was using this unpleasant situation to her own advantage. She worried to what extent the students had been harmed and what could be done about this situation after the fact.

This case has many dimensions. The manager was clearly not managing as closely as she needed to, probably because she had mistakenly trusted the supervisor. The supervisor's behaviour was unethical in that she had a responsibility to act on the information given to her by teachers and students, but failed to do so. The teachers' behaviour was unethical in the sense that they failed to put the students' interests ahead of their desire to not get involved. And as for the teacher, he was an unwell person who needed assistance but would not get it until he recognized his own neediness.

I have often experienced this misplaced loyalty on the part of teachers towards their colleagues. They feel it is against their code of ethics to "rat out" a fellow teacher. It appears that such individuals place more value on that "ethic" than they do on the well-being of the learners, who have entrusted their learning and well-being to that organization which the teachers are a part of. When I talk to teachers about problems in this regard, they have often seen my point and they realize that they have erred in their priorities. I have confidence that those teachers in this scenario would choose differently in the future. As for the supervisor, I remain puzzled by how she can justify protecting a wrong-doer just because he or she is a teacher. I hope that we will talk about this issue in teacher preparation programs and in professional development activities as I believe that teachers may make better choices if they think about these issues before they are confronted with an actual situation.

Suggested Principles for Designing a Code of Conduct

If a code of conduct is to be effective, it must have the ownership of those who will be governed by it. Therefore, professional associations, organizations, and individuals need to wrestle with these issues and come up with a set of principles they know the majority can live by. To that end, I offer some working principles to guide our thinking:

- That decisions regarding acceptable and unacceptable conduct by teachers and other staff members working with learners be based on what is in the best interests of learners, not on what is in the perceived best interests of individual staff members.
- That such decisions respect the historical, political, cultural, and religious diversity represented by the learners who study in our programs.
- That staff members be carefully advised, verbally and in writing, prior to beginning their employment, of the existence and details of an organizational code of conduct, and of the consequences of failing to adhere to it.

- That learners in programs be advised, if necessary in their own languages, as to the nature of the code of conduct they can expect from staff, and of what procedures they can follow if they feel a staff member is in violation of this code.
- That once a code of conduct has been accepted by an association or organization, violations to the code will be be acted upon firmly.

Potential Elements to Include in a Code of Conduct

- Relationships between staff and learners
- Relationships among staff members
- Limitations and conditions on receipt of gifts
- Responsibilities to learners if they witness violations to the code, and steps for addressing violations in a manner that is both fair to the staff person and to the learners
- Respect for learners, regardless of their values in relation to religion, politics, or other strongly held positions
- Right of learners to participate in decisions regarding their curriculum of studies
- Non-exploitation of learners (e.g., not using them to recruit, or selling raffle tickets, or other commercial products, or inviting them to events outside class time for personal reasons)
- Appropriate means of dealing with complaints regarding the employing organization
- Setting aside personal agendas in curriculum decisions
- Disclosure/non-disclosure of personal truths that may be overly distressing to learners

Workshop Activity

Using the guidelines above, and any others you can think of, write a personal code of conduct which you believe is appropriate for your teaching context. Better yet, join together with other teachers and do this as a group. Alternatively, present your code to a group of students and see what points they would like to add. If you feel strongly about this subject, approach your professional association to see if they have thought about working with their membership to prepare something for everyone. Controversial? Of course. Necessary? In the interests of the learners, absolutely.

CHAPTER 5

The Fourth Dimension

Questions to reflect upon:

- Thinking back to your own days as a student, which teacher or teachers made your heart sing? What was it about that person or people that enabled that experience, and what was it like?

- As a teacher, can you recall moments when your students were very happy in class? Can you remember moments when they were struggling to stay awake or when they seemed quite resistant? To what do you attribute the difference between the first instance and the second two?

- When you are really hurting inside, how do you want those around you to treat you? With sympathy? With compassion? Do you want people to just leave you alone and pretend everything is fine? Do you want them to offer suggestions or give you advice? Do others, in your experience, feel as you do or differently in this instance?

- In what ways have others contributed to your feelings of strength? Of weakness?

- Have you ever been in a community of people, if only for an instant, where you felt totally at one with the universe: peaceful, happy, elated, and connected? If so, how do you account for that experience and for the fact that it is not always present?

Our scientific worldview has too often left us trying to believe that we are merely physical, mental, and emotional beings. Many of us experience this three-dimensional view as wanting. We are creatures who seek to understand the meaning of life and of events that befall us and others in the world. We seek to be connected to something greater than ourselves, and we often experience the mystery of life when we least expect it. In the ESL classroom with its multiplicity of cultures, languages, and historical experiences, we are offered a virtual banquet of possibilities by which we can understand these perspectives as they manifest themselves in different people and communities. It is to these yearnings and experiences that I apply the term "fourth dimension."

The Fourth Dimension: What Is It? What Is It Not?

While I speak about the "fourth dimension," I am undoubtedly talking about the place of spirituality in the classroom—I am absolutely not talking about religion in the classroom. Religion is the institutionalization of spiritual experience. While religions have given their members a sense of certainty and comfort in relation to life's big questions, they have also served, in many cases, to divide people. All too often people believe that in order for them to hold the tenets of their own faith, they have to reject the tenets of someone else's. In ESL, religion *can* be an obstacle. (It can also be the "Rock of Gibraltar" for learners in a difficult time.) Extremely religious teachers sometimes see no conflict of interest in trying to recruit learners to their particular brand of truth. Extremely religious learners sometimes feel no sense of imposition in trying to convert fellow students or staff to their particular brand of truth. Both of those instances are far from what I want to discuss in this chapter.

Perhaps a short story will better illustrate where I am trying to go with this topic. Some years ago, while working with immigrant adult newcomers in a large institution, I remember doing the initial placement test for a radiant, older Russian man who had a wonderful sense of humour and absolutely no English whatsoever. Our placement tests were designed to find the level for those students who had some English skills, or, in cases where they were absolute beginners, to find out whether or not they were literate in their own languages and how quickly they learned new information. In trying to communicate with this man, I experienced his energy and passion for life. He shrugged off the obvious hilarity of not understanding one word I said, but quickly tuned into my body language and tried to understand what I was asking of him in that situation. I placed him in a fast-moving beginners' class and wished him well. He was a delightful and charming man, and I thought he would do very well.

About three months later, I saw a pale, slowly moving man dejectedly walking down the hallway. At first, I did not recognize him. He looked so much older than he had before. Then, he looked up and I saw those unmistakably blue eyes, but it was as if the light had gone out in them. Astonished, I greeted him and tried to talk with him. He seemed to understand me and uttered a few words of very broken English before he slowly turned away. I was shocked and very sad at his apparent change for the worse.

I found out who his teacher was and spoke to her about my observations. She had also noticed the gradual but certain change from a healthy, passionate, self-confident individual to one who had lost hope in life. She had no explanation for this change except to say that he found language learning difficult and was very frustrated not to be able to communicate with the people around him. In the USSR, this man had been an engineer—he was obviously well-educated. Why, I wondered, was he finding learning so much more difficult than his peers? I felt helpless and could not help but wish he were in my class where I would at least have a chance to find that old sparkle in his eyes and to get him laughing again.

This man had his physical needs met. A government-sponsored refugee, he had a one year's allowance from the government to get established. He was being mentally stimulated with this new language and the need to reconnect, emotionally and intellectually, to people around him. How do we explain his response to loss? For me, his spirit was seriously depleted. He had lost his sense of dignity, and the longer he was in Canada, the more he believed he was too old to ever regain it. Suddenly a man who had been respected and had a complete circle of acquaintances was now "an immigrant," a student stumbling to learn the basics of a language like a child. Because he was in his fifties, he felt he did not have time to learn and get a good job. It no doubt also pained him to watch his family struggling with their own integration and to feel powerless to prevent that struggle for them. This man had left more than his country. In his own eyes, he had left behind everything that was his identity. He was in some sense a lost pilgrim on life's journey.

The compassionate educator's response to such a one has got to be more than lessons in grammar and vocabulary. This man, like the Turkish-Cypriot woman in our earlier story, needed to laugh. He needed to re-experience joy in his days, and in that joy, he would find hope that the future held meaning for him. He needed to feel respected and valued for who he was and had been. All he saw were his errors and the teacher's many corrections. A man who had once seen himself as intelligent now saw himself as stupid. The contrast was unbearable. I am always saddened when I hear a student say, "Before I came to this class, I did not know how much I didn't know. Now, I do."

In trying to understand these discouraged students, I look to my own contrasting experiences as a second language learner. I remember years of trying to learn French, especially in Quebec, and of taking papers home that had taken me hours to write, only to get them back covered in red ink—as if there were blood dripping finely all over the page. I could not read the teacher's hastily written corrections, and there were so many of them. I could not possibly absorb all the potential learnings, even if I could have read them. I hated to write and I hated to get my assignments back. I hesitated to speak to anyone in French because I was afraid they would think less of me for making so many errors.

Years later, I spent a month in Chile after having taken only five lessons in Spanish (from which I remembered sweet "nada"). My natural curiosity, not to mention my survival instincts (Pinochet was very much in power at that time), ensured that I asked lots of questions and that I actually remembered most of the answers. In one month, I learned a lot, probably because it was a real-life situation and because I had no one around with whom to speak English. Nor did I have any learned fear of speaking Spanish. I didn't care about my mistakes because no one reacted to them. The Chileans I met simply wanted to understand me—and me them.

Some years later, when I was working with Korean teachers every summer in a Teacher Education project, I decided it would be nice to learn some Korean, and I registered for classes. Aieeeyaieeyaiee! The teacher was an older man, a minister, who seemed[1] to me at the time to know nothing at all about teaching, and certainly nothing about how Canadians taught and learned second languages. His idea of teaching was to give us a printed lesson, read it aloud, and give us the chance to repeat what he said, and then send us home to memorize it. We had a grand total of two lessons to learn the entire Korean writing system (which is like an alphabet except the letters are combined in groups of three per syllable, and they change shape according to what they are being combined with, and in what order). We were expected to be able to write and say these letters as they appeared in words. I spent hours memorizing them and got so that I could "read" aloud quite well. The only problem was, I did not have a clue what any of it meant, and my writing made all the Korean children in the class laugh because it was even more childlike than theirs. (Printing has never been my strong suit.) In frustration with this method of teaching and my shortage of time, I quit the class and cannot now remember even one letter of the writing system that I once read aloud with relative ease.

So, what do I make of all this? My spirit was nurtured by the relationships I was able to form in Spanish and by all the knowledge I wanted to gain in that language. I had never lived in a land as oppressed as Chile was at that time. I wanted to know about the bodies in the river, about the helicopters flying so low over our heads, about why we couldn't congregate in big groups; about why the young people at the irrigation canal did not want the old grandmother telling me, a stranger, all the things the government had done to her family. Spanish was the

---

1 I say "seemed" because that is how it struck me at the time. I have since come to respect the varied cultural approaches to teaching and learning (each of which is more or less effective within the culture where it is practised). Jill Bell wrote an interesting dissertation on this topic, Becoming Aware of Literary. (See Bibliography.)

medium which helped me make connections with some wonderful, interesting people who were making the best of some hard times.

French was, when all was said and done, primarily a book language to me. Only for the brief time I spent in Quebec, when I went to the restaurants, took the taxis, and shopped in the stores, was it a real language with real people. Korean was the end of that same continuum. To me it was a language of torture, a language in which I could not possibly be successful, and where I was laughed at.

As an educator, I have seen different students learn differently. We are each a product of the ways in which we have learned and of the healthy or unhealthy views we have developed of ourselves and of others. Those circumstances condition how we are able to learn in new situations. In general, I believe, students learn best when they feel respected and liked, when they are relaxed and happy, when their basic personal needs are being met, and when what they are learning is experienced as relevant and important, both to the present moment and to the future. A plumber in my class flat out told me he could care less about verb tenses. He wanted to learn the names of the tools of his trade and of the problems he would be asked to fix as a plumber. That was all he was open to learning, and it was very important to him that he learn this vocabulary as soon as possible so that he could get a job and take care of his family. Few learners are that clear about what they want to learn or are that inflexible, but when they are, it is a gift because we know exactly what we have to do to satisfy them.

The fourth dimension, then, is about nourishing the spirits of the learners in our classes; finding ways for them to rediscover joy and laughter in their new language, inspiring hope and self-confidence in each person, and recognizing the need for human beings to experience education as a healing activity, when it is appropriate.

Acknowledging and Restoring the Spiritual Dimension Within Ourselves

Many teachers seem to know intuitively what is most important to learners. The best teachers I have seen throughout my career are those whose students find themselves laughing a lot in the classroom and at the same time learning that which is relevant to their lives. When I have surveyed students in order to discover what qualities they deem to be the most important qualities they would look for—if *they* were hiring a prospective teacher, they do not say "a teaching certificate, TESL training, or years of experience." Almost always, they say they want a person who is friendly, happy, and energetic, or words to that effect. These same students who laugh so heartily in class during the day may confess to crying a lot at home in the evening as they release their fears, frustrations, and sorrow. For the intuitive teacher, there is no need to understand why laughter is important, for it comes automatically. These teachers know the difference between laughing *at* someone, which is devastating, and laughing *with* someone, which often starts when the teacher is able to laugh at herself. For teachers not blessed with these kinds of intuitions or who have personalities more inclined to being serious, it is important to understand intellectually why hope, joy, and the other aspects of spirituality are such important parts in the "lived" curriculum of a language learner.

I have long believed that effective teaching happens when it springs from the common ground we find with our students. If I am to understand how a learner feels when hope is abandoned, I need to identify with some similar type of experience myself. Likewise, to help a learner recover from loss, I need to understand loss in my own life, and how to recover and go forward following the experience of such loss. When we can find our common ground and respond to learners from this place, especially if we personally have moved beyond the negativity of such experiences in our own lives, using them to make ourselves stronger, we then understand that it is not sympathy which benefits a learner in these situations but rather strength and faith.

Many years ago, I remember doing some story work with a group of women in a job training program, and for whatever reason, most of the stories that day were profoundly sad and depressing. We were all deeply shaken by what everyone had shared, and we all felt overwhelmed and teary. One astute learner walked quietly to my side and said, "Please, Virginia, do not allow both of your feet to wade into this river with us. We need you to keep one foot on the safety of the bank." I understood immediately what she was telling me: I was not to let my sadness sweep me into their river of sadness, for that would simply leave all of us drowning in tears together. By greeting their stories with respect rather than with horror and helplessness, I could be present to help them find their own strength to deal with past negative experiences that were still laying claim to their thoughts and emotions.

We can only assist others with their healing if we are willing to heal ourselves. If we have repressed our own negative emotions and allowed them to make us ill, or to separate us from the people around us, we will have no ability or desire to be present to others who need to face their own demons. The theologian Henri Noewen in his lovely book *The Wounded Healer* speaks beautifully of this connection between our own healing journeys and our ability to work successfully with others in theirs.

If anyone thinks I am suggesting that we should all become counsellors, I am not. Counselling, as we understand that term, is only one model of supporting people in healing wounded lives. Ministry is another. Some theologians promote a theology of presence in ministry, and I find this concept equally applicable in education. I believe in a pedagogy of presence. To be present with another is not to push him this way or that. It is not to advise him or counsel him. It is simply to be there with him in strength, in faith, in hope, and in fact.

When my son was killed in an accident, our lives were turned upside down. I have never known deeper darkness and despair than I did that first year. All my perceptions were affected. I would never be the same person again. At that time, I expected my friends to be present to my suffering and healing. In some cases, that was true and in others it was not. Some people I knew very well had no common ground with which to experience what we were going through and dealt with their own horror by avoiding me. Others whom I did not even know, but who had had common experiences were very present to me, and I shall be eternally grateful for the sanity they brought me during this insane time. I remember one woman I had just met who came to me and said simply, "I don't know what to do for you, but I want to do something. Please, if there is anything I can do, just ask." I looked at her and saw that she was genuine. I said, "Could you drive me to the airport Friday night?" She smiled and agreed. She was happy and I felt supported. It was a small thing, but it meant I was not alone. In other words, it was not what a person did that was important, but that they did something. That is what it means to be present.

Most of us will never know what a person goes through during war, (thank goodness), or how difficult it is to leave one's country and settle anew. However, we can find other experiences in our lives which provide parallel kinds of emotions, different losses, different frustrations, different alienations, and from those experiences we can try to understand what the learner is feeling. From that place, we can learn to be present in the small interactions with individuals and with the decisions we make in regard to curriculum and materials.

Welcoming the Fourth Dimension into the Classroom

Please do not read this chapter as if it were a new technique for doing ESL. It is not. These ideas will not suit everyone. I share my thoughts with those to whom they make sense. If they do not make sense to you, then by all means stick to what does. For each of us should do what we do well in the classroom and not try to do anything that feels uncomfortable or strange to us. To teach well is to teach from the centre of our being—not to apply techniques that work well for others but do not fit for us.

If you find yourself agreeing with much of what I have said, you may also be asking how you can develop your classrooms to be more welcoming of the spiritual dimensions of education. The foundation of spirituality, as I envision it, is to be genuinely respectful of each and every learner who comes your way. That is easier said than done.

I remember meeting a woman on Cortes Island (one of the Gulf Islands off the coast of Vancouver Island), who was there to teach Tai Chi. This woman, though diminutive in stature, was a very large person in spirit. Wherever she walked in her serenely happy manner, heads turned and people smiled shyly at her. She was genuinely respectful of each person she met, and that struck me as sufficiently unusual and it made quite an impression. I delighted in watching her as she would acknowledge each person on her path, sometimes stopping to talk and sometimes just smiling and moving on. It seemed that wherever she walked, she left peaceful vibes in her wake.

I have long contemplated what made this woman so unusual and why she had made such an impression on me. I know she had gone to Japan and lived in a monastery for some years. What had she discovered there that the rest of us did not know? I can only surmise that she learned what many religious leaders have taught us for centuries—that we are all one. In celebrating the life of a stranger, she was celebrating her own life. In bringing happiness to others, she brought happiness to herself. When we force ourselves to treat others with apparent respect, regardless of our feelings—that is toleration, not respect, and it is easily seen through. To communicate respect for another, we must first find it within ourselves.

I have also found *story* a powerful tool in ESL classrooms. By that I mean the telling and sharing of true and significant moments in our lives. Each time we tell a story, we bind our experience. That means that as our attitude towards our experiences shifts, our stories will change too. When we tell a story, we decide what to tell and what to ignore or keep secret. Our manner of telling reveals a great deal about us to our listeners. It is, therefore, an intimate act.

Janet Gunn in her book *Autobiography: Towards a Poetics of Experience* refers to the autobiography as a presencing, in Augustine's words, "of man in his deep." She goes on to say that, "What is made present is not merely a past that is past. What is presenced is a reality, always new, to which the past has contributed but which stands, as it were, in front of the autobiographer. To lay claim to one's life, and thereby to become "fierce with reality" is to understand that reality as something to which one is continually trying to catch up. . . ." What a wonderful notion, that of ESL learners becoming fierce with reality.

I have no difficulty getting learners to share their stories. There are many, many ways of doing that. What I have had difficulty with through the years is knowing what to do with some of the stories when they are told. Often, there is no need to do anything. The telling alone has done what it needed to do: it has freed the teller from the need to hide painful thoughts, or it has shown the teller to be a person of humour and wit, or it has connected the teller to the listener, who now knows the storyteller in a different way.

Occasionally, however, a story carries with it a strong sense of unfinished business. The teller is not reconciled with the events of the story and appears in its telling to be seeking a way to do so. I remember one learner who spoke during a story circle of being sexually molested by a doctor in a hospital. At the time she spoke no English to tell anyone and knew that if she told her husband, he would kill the man—not report him. She had never told anyone that story in the twelve years since it had happened.

I asked her if she wanted to do anything about this incident now. She was horrified and said no, as this man was quite prominent in her community, and revealing what had happened would only make trouble for her family, particularly after all this time. She said she felt better just having shared it and having others share her sense of profound injustice and anger at this exploitation of his power. She felt that this event had continued to mark her in her relationships with men in this society. She was very shy, fearful, and angry. This learner knew she needed to work through this trauma outside of classroom, either in her own way or with the help of a professional. In addition, I was then left with a sense of gnawing responsibility, not just to her, but to the dozens or maybe hundreds of women who might yet be molested by this man. I was torn. On the one hand, I respected this woman's trust and would not do anything to push her one way or the other. On the other hand, he needed to be stopped.

Like the woman above, people share stories because it feels good to "vent." Here, I have trouble knowing what to do when I can see clearly the actions such a person can take to change those situations which are giving them distress; I know not what to do when the person appears unwilling to take any action to change very destructive situations for either their benefit or the benefit of their families. With great difficulty, I have decided to choose the path of allowing each individual to live with his or her decisions, and not try to convince anyone to do anything. Life's mysteries are beyond me, and surely it is enough that I discover what I can do to become accountable for my own life and leave others to make their own choices. This is where my own faith steps in, and I have to assume that I do not need to save the world by myself. (And yes, that sounds sufficiently ridiculous—that I am forced to laugh at my own presumptuousness in ever assuming that I could know what was best for anyone in any case.)

Stories do more than release stress for the teller. They allow us to learn vicariously from one another's experiences. They allow us to find common themes and thereby enhance our understanding of the world around us. And through better understanding, we can all make more informed choices. Stories are also community builders.

Many teachers have taken to doing journal work with their students, and while this practise can be very positive for some learners, it can also be very negative. If journals are graded, they have become an exercise rather than a sharing, and the opportunity is lost. If journals are corrected as a matter of course, they can become an object of torment for the one who is already hitting herself over the head for being slow.

If, instead, the journals are a dialogue, these writings can provide a valuable opportunity for learners to establish a one-on-one communication with a native speaker. Each person can be encouraged to make the journal what he or she needs it to be. Some learners will ask their teachers to correct language errors in spelling, verb tenses, or word order. Others will use their journals to explore dangerous topics they would not feel comfortable discussing in the classroom.

Beware, however, because one of the possible spinoffs of keeping the journals private between the teacher and the individual is that mistrust can develop in the classroom. If one student, rightly or wrongly, believes that another is complaining or gossiping about him or her in the journals, and that does happen, right away the relationships in the classroom have become unequal. If one wants a participatory classroom where a strong experience of community is present for all, this is inconsistent with private journals.

When one does structured verbal story work, I suggest using the *Rule of Invitation* and the *Rule of Confidentiality*. The Rule of Invitation means that no one feels obligated to do anything that makes him or her feel uncomfortable. The latter rule means that what is said in the room stays in the room, and that the storytelling exercise does not begin until every individual has contracted to that agreement.

Workshop Activity

Recall a time when you were a student in a classroom and going through a difficult time, or just feeling upset about something that had happened. Recall the details of that experience—who was there, what were you doing, how did you feel. What was the teacher like? Could he or she recognize that you were upset or were you able to hide it? If he or she was aware of your state of mind, did the teacher respond in some way or ignore it? How did you feel about that? Is there anything to be learned from this experience? You may wish to write about this experience and your reflections upon it. This activity will obviously be of greater value if it is done by a number of people and shared.

Participatory Education:
A Critical Alternative

Questions to reflect upon:

- In general, do you prefer to be told what to do or to determine that for yourself?
- In what kinds of learning situations do you prefer to be quite directed?
- When you recall your own schooling, what do you remember most about various periods therein?
- Do you believe that you can make the world a better place? For yourself? For others?
- When you look at a picture, do you see the same thing as someone else who is looking at that picture? When you hear a song that reminds you of someone special in your life, do you hear that song in the same way as someone else who did not share that experience with you? Why is this?
- Do you see yourself primarily as a recipient of knowledge, a creator of knowledge, or both?

The renowned Princeton physicist John Wheeler writes: "We used to think of the universe as 'out there,' to be observed as it were from behind the screen of a foot-thick slab of glass, safely, without personal involvement. The truth, quantum theory tells us, is quite different. . . . The observer is increasingly promoted to participator. In some strange sense, this is a participatory universe." (Quoted in *Unconditional Life: Discovering the Power to Fulfill Your Dreams*, Deepak Chopra)

What Is Participatory Education?

Participatory education is an alternative to the delivery-based approaches to education that have dominated our field for some time. In order to clarify our understanding of the differences between these two radically different approaches to the teaching of English as a Second or Foreign Language, let us compare them:

Delivery-Based Training VS. Participatory Education: A Comparison

	Delivery-Based Training	Participatory Education
Preliminary knowledge	Knowledge about learners and what they need to learn is assumed to be sufficient before program begins.	It is assumed that we do not have sufficient knowledge of the learners to know precisely what they need to learn or how they can best learn it, and that we need the actual learners' involvement in determining both.
Role of the learner	Learner is a passive recipient of predetermined knowledge.	Learner is an active participant in sharing and creating knowledge as well as evaluating learning.
	Objects of instruction.	Agents of social change.
Role of the teacher	An expert in charge of delivering the program and in determining success or failure of learner to learn within it.	A facilitator responsible for maximizing opportunities for all participants to share what they know and to work together to create new knowledge that will benefit the lives of themselves and the community.

	Delivery-Based Training	Participatory Education
Purpose of program	*Goals* are determined by staff members prior to beginning of program. The success or failure of the learner is determined by the measurable achievement of these goals.	*Intents* form the general direction of program planned by staff before commencement of program, but are open to major changes as identified by participants at any time during the program. Success or failure of the program is determined by satisfaction of all participants. (Staff and learners are all considered participants.)
Understanding of language	*Language* is a complex tool used by human beings to communicate with one another.	*Language* is the medium of communication, knowledge-making, and human experience.
Understanding of education and training	Training exists to ensure that learners have the opportunity to acquire the skills that have been identified by those with authority as essential to those learners for a particular purpose (e.g., settlement, work, further study).	Education exists to enable individuals to fulfill their potential, as individuals and as a community.
Curriculum	A document which outlines what is to be learned, within what time frames, with what resources.	Curriculum has two faces: the plan and the lived experience. Each aspect of the curriculum is dynamic and responsive to the other.

	Delivery-Based Training	Participatory Education
Resources	Texts are the authority for learning and are used, for the most part, unquestioningly.	All resources are used critically. Learners are encouraged to consider the backgrounds of those who prepared materials and their motivations for doing so. Many learning materials are produced by learners.
Activities	Generally decided by teacher.	Negotiated with participants.
Power	Power resides in hierarchical structures with teacher over learners, administrator over teacher.	Power is shared among participants and exercised for the good of the community, as well as for the individual participants.
Evaluation	Students are evaluated according to predetermined benchmarks of success. The program is evaluated to determine its success in meeting the goals. Teachers are evaluated to determine their success in delivering the program. Program is primarily accountable to those who fund it.	Evaluation is an on-going attitude of valuing what is taking place and making adjustments for improvements. Program is primarily accountable to participants.

	Delivery-Based Training	Participatory Education
Culture	In general, culture is assumed to be transmittable to learners.	Culture is negotiable. Participants look critically at what each has experienced and choose consciously what seems most attractive and appropriate.
Time frame	Because the body of knowledge is clearly known, a time frame is chosen in which the majority of learners can acquire the knowledge and skills identified.	Any predetermination of time frame would be arbitrary in that individual learners require different amounts of time to learn specific things. Participatory education is by definition open-ended. Ideally, participants would themselves determine when they wanted to exit a program or conclude it.
Learner's relationship to teacher and other learners	The learner is primarily responsible to him or herself. Learner ensures that he/she does not interfere with the learning of others or with the teacher's instruction.	All participants are accountable for themselves but responsible to one another. Each person shares what expertise he or she can to the collective learning.
Worldview	The world is out there awaiting discovery and mastery. Education helps us to understand the world and control it.	The world is as we make it. The world can be a better place and education can help us make it so.

	Delivery-Based Training	Participatory Education
Values	Values are often presumed rather than overtly stated, or, when they are stated, are often inconsistent with other aspects of the curriculum documents.	Values are seen as very important, with the awareness that most values are unconscious, and we need to discover what the operative values are in our lives and in whose interests they serve.
In whose interest	Programs are delivered in the interest of the status quo for example, to provide labour for the workforce or to get welfare recipients off the public purse.	Programs are offered in the interests of the community as a whole, which means taking into account those whose voices are not currently heard in that community.
Voice	Learners learn to speak the voice in which they are expected to speak: polite, obedient, and in accord with the expectations of authority.	Learners learn to find their own voice and speak to be heard in order to address issues of injustice and inequality where they exist.
Vision	The world is basically fine, as is, and learners must learn to fit into it.	The world is not fine as is, and learners can learn in order to identify what is wrong, envision ways of making it better, and act to make it so.

It would be easy to look at this comparison and say that ESL is not an appropriate context in which to do participatory education. If you have found yourself saying that, let me suggest a compromise. Most of our programs are bounded by funding guidelines and time frames that never seem long enough to do what we believe needs to be done. Indeed if one wanted to stick rigidly to the right-hand column, we would almost have to be independently wealthy to facilitate such a program. Actually, participatory education has come to us from *popular education* where facilitators were often volunteers working in their communities to improve very difficult life situations. Paolo Freire is the best known educator of this kind. He recognized the political nature of education. He knew that education was necessarily rooted in values and that, when we were unconscious of those values, we were necessarily acting to reproduce the status quo.

The fact is that we live in an unjust world, a world in which some countries have disproportionate access to wealth while others are desperate to keep their people from starving to death, a world in which, even within wealthy countries, the rich have access to resources such as learning, while the poor do not. Many of us have convinced ourselves that those who work hard have what they need, and those who are lazy do not. But, if we believe that, we have not allowed ourselves to get to know the working poor or the generations of people on social assistance. In the province where I live, there are many families where two adults work full-time (some in two or more jobs), but the family still needs social assistance to meet their basic needs.

Delivery-based education is based on a lot of assumptions about what people need to be successful in life. We are still churning out occupational profiles, essential skills matrixes, and adult competency frameworks as if we understood what learners need to be successful in life—as if we could possibly understand what others need, when their lives are profoundly different from our own. In all of these costly and time-consuming endeavours, we have not asked the learners what they have needed and wanted. If we did, we might be surprised at some of the answers. We might hear words like, "respect and dignity, an opportunity to be heard, a chance to better myself, courses that accommodate shift workers, courses that are free because we do not have enough money to pay."

Nor do most of us seek to understand how it is that many learners find themselves in the situations they do. We are all to some degree products of our parents, our extended families, and the historical and cultural condition of our communities. We are only somewhat conscious of how we acquired our values and attitudes. Our attitudes towards possibility, in particular, are learned attitudes. One of the reasons that slavery was tolerated so long was because many people believed that this economic arrangement was the natural order of things, or that those who were enslaved had no power to do anything about it. It was only when people named evil for what it was, and elected to do whatever it took to abolish that evil—that change was made possible. Change began with the expectation that life could be better.

Furthermore, in deciding what can and should be learned in an educational program, it is not even a question of knowing what someone else needs. Put the shoe on your own foot. Do you want someone else telling you what you need, or how you should go about getting it within a time frame? Or, would you prefer to discover that for yourself and make it happen for yourself? We all need the expertise of others in our learning, but we like a certain sense of power in determining how we use that expertise. We do not want it dumped on us without any consideration of what is important to us. Any time an authority takes charge of someone else's learning, the learner is forced into a position of passivity. Whatever else that person learns, he also learns that he is a receptacle. Any sense that he is not capable of knowing what he needs or of making it happen is reinforced by such modes of learning which separate the "experts" from those who are "deficient," which focus not on who a person is or what he is capable of becoming but simply on what he lacks. This approach to education is essentially a dehumanizing one.

Instead of saying it is all or nothing in relation to these ideas, let us instead ask ourselves if we are teaching in a context where we could begin with an *attitude* of participatory education. Let's see if we could start with a few of the basic understandings outlined in the preceding chart. If we can see the desirability of learners having meaningful input into what and how they learn, we can find small ways to do that in any program. We can give choices. We can invite opinions.

Here is a very simple illustration of the power of these ideas. All of us in ESL have at one time or another used pictures in our teaching. "What is this?" "What is that?" "What is he doing?" "What colour is the _____?" One day, I had two student teachers coming in to observe a class, and I was planning to use pictures in my lesson. Instead of asking very specific questions about the pictures, I decided to ask just one question, "What do you see in this picture?" and invited the students to ask each other this question. I had nine pictures posted at the front of the room. To my amazement, the students did not "see" what I saw in the pictures. What they saw was conditioned by their experiences, just as what I saw was conditioned by mine. When I looked at one picture, I saw a bright summer blue sky with a field of beautiful, yellow flowers gently waving in the breeze. It made me happy, and just by looking at it, I could smell that warm pollen smell of summer and hear the bees buzzing in the flowers. I felt the warmth of the sun upon my skin, and I radiated with happiness—a beautiful picture, for me.

For one woman in the class, however, it was a scene of great pain, and she wept as she described a similar field where several people had been rounded up and shot. She would never look at this picture and see beauty. She saw only blood, death, and pain.

Other pictures that looked fairly nondescript to me were viewed with joy by the learners. One man, looking at a path around a lake, remembered better times when he and his wife had cycled regularly in their country, and had a lot of fun together. Someone else looking at the same picture saw a lake where he used to picnic with his children when they were small; for him, all those happy memories were in the picture. The two student teachers, who had come to observe, were as drawn into the discussion as I was and quickly forgot their intent to "just observe." They jumped in with their experiences of the pictures and became in every sense participants in the class, even as I had done that day.

My intent in doing that lesson long ago had been to introduce vocabulary and to practise grammar. The results were so much more significant. We all learned the degree to which perception conditions our seeing and experiencing of life. If I had done the usual ESL "thing" of asking specific information questions, none of us would have had the experience we did, or would have gotten to know one another as intimately as we did that day.

When to Use Which Approach

To decide which approach to learning is appropriate for you to use depends on several factors. First of all, it depends on how you see your role and the role of the program in which you teach. If the left column of the chart seems more appropriate right down the line, then it probably is. If the right column feels better to you, then it probably is.

A basic question to ask yourself is how you see the role of the immigrant in society. If you believe that immigrants come to this country because they want to become like the mainstream, then a training (delivery) method is definitely more appropriate. If you believe that immigrants have as much to teach us as we do them, then participatory education is a more appropriate approach to follow. In both cases, the learners are learning language. The biggest difference is that, in training, the teacher has largely predetermined *what* language is learned, and in participatory learning, language is the medium rather than the focus of what is being learned. In training, knowledge is being transmitted. In participatory education, it is being created.

One situation in which training is preferred to participatory education is when very specific content must be learned within a specified time frame. An example would be TOEFL preparation. The TOEFL examination is a standardized test that must be written in several countries in order for English as a second language speakers to gain university entrance. There is no negotiating on this point. Either they get the requisite score, usually about 600, or they are rejected. Some students in TOEFL preparation classes may have tried the test before, but many others may not have. They are depending on the instructor and the materials to do whatever it takes to get them through that test successfully. It is appropriate, in this instance, to predetermine exactly what content needs to be covered and how.

Another example where the training approach is more appropriate, would be a job training program wherein specific skills and content knowledge must be learned in order for the participants to qualify for and work safely and effectively in a particular job. In this kind of a program, there can be components that are negotiable, but certain other components are not. When the organization where I was director for ten years, offered job training programs, we always made sure there was at least one course with a great deal of built-in flexibility (where learners could say what was on their minds and make choices about what they wanted to learn and how). Sometimes, we called the course "Canadian Experience." Our intent was to give learners a chance to talk about aspects of their Canadian experience that had been confusing, frustrating, or problematic to them in some way. We tried to address the learners' need for understanding and skills to meet such concerns and problems where they arose. Learners told stories, especially ones that were about previous workplace experiences, which served to teach the whole group. The less power a worker is perceived to have in the workplace, the more vulnerable her or she is to exploitation and/or abuse. Things happen to immigrant workers that we find hard to believe if they have never happened to us: racial epithets hurled, failure to receive overtime wages with a threat of dismissal if the worker says anything; or being set up by another employee who feels threatened by an immigrant worker's competence, for example. Immigrants also deal with sexual harassment, male chauvinism, the devastating effects of gossip, and the other kinds of negative experiences that many of us have encountered before. Stories told by someone you know, whether it is a fellow student or a staff member, somehow carry much more weight in our minds than a teacher's lecture advising us of what might happen.

Some aspects of the workplace that we take for granted may seem very strange to someone from another culture. One woman got exactly the job placement she had asked for—assistant cook in a nursing home kitchen—only to be terribly offended when she arrived and learned that men worked in the same kitchen. As a conservative Moslem woman, she had assumed she would be sent to a work area where there were no men. She had to leave the placement because in her culture it was considered most inappropriate for men and women to work in the same area. She said her husband would never allow it.

Another woman, who was from India, was in tears every night because her fellow workers in a kitchen restaurant used "swear words." Our staff person, who was familiar with the staff at the restaurant, characterized them as very nice, but a little rough around the edges. Perhaps, if this woman had had a context to understand the place of profanity in our society, she would not have taken it so personally. We wondered if her birth family had been a privileged one, as she seemed unaccustomed to the behaviour of working people.

The beauty of participatory education is that this approach can take all the experiences and observations participants have had and use them to fashion a curriculum where language is learned, along with culture and all sorts of information about the community.

In that discussion is used a great deal in participatory education programs, many teachers believe this approach can work only when learners have attained a high level of language development, but I have found that this is not entirely true. To be sure, there has to be some language and the early stages of learning are necessarily teachers directed to some degree, but learners can participate from the very beginning if they are given the tools to do so. If a group of learners is given the following basic questions to use from the beginning of their learning, they can quickly take responsibility for what comes next:

- What does _____ mean?
- How do you spell _____?
- I don't understand. Would you repeat that please?
- What is this/that? What are these/those?
- How do you say this word?

These basic questions become the tools of language learning. They can be introduced early on in the course and mounted on a poster at the front of the classroom to remind people how to use them. Additional expressions can be added as needed.

I have done story work with learners who had very little vocabulary. These learners were motivated by having something important to share, and were assisted by other learners in the classroom who spoke their language and could help them find the words. Students use body language and pictures to say what they are trying to say. Such ESL classes become like grand games of charades, except that what people are trying to say is real and important to them.

Starting Points to Participatory Education

I have found that a lot of teachers were very interested in participatory approaches, but because they had not experienced this type of education themselves, did not know where to begin. Here are some suggestions.

A. *Continually question yourself and your own attitudes.* We have been conditioned by hierarchical structures both in our educational systems and in our society as a whole. The only way to break free of those structures is to become aware of them and consciously choose otherwise. I found it very helpful to work with a colleague who had not gone through a typical schooling experience. Because everything was foreign to her, she questioned everything. Her attitude helped me discern what I was doing on autopilot and what I was choosing to do.

B. *Get to know your learners as individuals and give them opportunities to know one another as such.* This suggestion is not as obvious as one might think. People do not automatically trust one another nor do they trust, if having trusted, they have been "shot down" in some way. When a learner tries to say something in the classroom and the teacher says, "Could we stick to the topic please?," it is not likely that learner will be in a hurry to initiate something again. That kind of request is one we have probably all made in our programs and sometimes have to make if we are to cover material in the time given; we are not always conscious of the consequences.

C. *Don't rush learners when they are trying to formulate a thought.* We rush them in a dozen different ways: by looking impatient, by finishing their sentences for them, by asking the unspoken question rather than pointing to the poster or otherwise giving them a chance to come up with it themselves, by saying, "Yes?" in that special way that says, "I am waiting . . ." Such behaviour on our part tells the learners that their thoughts are less important than ours and not worth waiting for.

D. *Be prepared to disagree with decisions the learners make and be prepared to live with the consequences.* If a teacher gives learners choices and then vetoes those choices, no one will trust her again when she asks for participation. If you are not prepared to live with the learners' choice, do not give them that power to begin with.

E. *Ask open-ended questions rather than specific questions.* Instead of "What is she doing in this picture?," ask "What do you see in this picture?" Instead of "Do you like pizza?," ask "What foods do you like?"

F. *When you ask questions, make sure they are* real *questions.* By that I mean, only ask questions you genuinely want the answers to. Likewise, encourage learners to ask real questions and do not settle for questions that are composed to satisfy a particular grammar point (unless of course they have asked you about a particular point and you are looking for examples). I have no patience with workbooks that ask, "Does Bill Smith play tennis?" under a picture of a man swinging a racquet, because none of us knows who Bill Smith is or cares. On the other hand, we may well want to ask, "Do you play tennis?" and encourage learners to ask one another questions of this nature (which hopefully would be followed one day with other questions such as: "Would you like to come play with me one day after class?") Real language connects people and makes things happen. Artificial language puts us to sleep.

G. *Choose materials that the learners can relate to.* Teachers in developing countries have often had to contend with donated textbooks from countries where the people, the geography, and everything else bears little, if any, resemblance to the learners and their environment. When you have no choice as to what materials are available, either use them critically or have the learners make their own: photostories, shared experience stories, posters. By using the materials critically, I mean asking learners to think about who made the materials and for what purpose. Ask them, "Do you see yourself in these pictures?" or "Why not?" In the book *Getting There: Producing Photostories with Immigrant Women* written by Deborah Barndt, dian marino, and Ferne Cristall, the authors show how immigrant women felt about riding the Toronto subway, when all the women in the advertisements tended to be young, white, and beautiful. Nowadays, we see women of colour in the ads, but they are still young and beautiful, and they are still portrayed all too often for their sexuality rather than for their intellect or other talents.

In that many ESL/EFL materials are prepared for educated learners with money who can afford to ski, go to movies, party on the weekend, and go jogging to stay fit, these learning materials are inappropriate for use with women who work all day and then go home to cook and clean for their families. These learners cannot identify with the characters in these books and must wonder what life would be like if they could be like those characters.

H. *Do what you can to honour the learners' requests: go to a particular place, have a particular guest speaker, or use a particular book.* Even if you do not think that their request is as important as something you have planned, if the group thinks it is, and you accept their choice, you are teaching them that their ideas are valuable and that you respect their choices. Like we all do, they will learn the consequences of their own choices and grow from them. The more often their choices are honoured, the more often they will be willing to make them.

I. *Do on-going evaluation rather than waiting until the end of a class, a unit, or a session.* And instead of asking people if something is good, fair, or poor, for example, ask them what they learned that was important and why. Do not settle for vague answers. If someone says, "I learned vocabulary today," ask them to tell you which word they learned and why it is important to them. If they say they learned grammar today, ask them which structure they learned and how knowing this structure will make a difference to them. This process is not easy to do initially because students will give you the answers they think you want to hear namely, the things that they have been told learning English was all about. It is only when they know it is safe to tell the truth that they will begin to do so.

J. *Present problems and ask the learners to tell you how they would respond to these scenarios if confronted with them.* Encourage them to tell you if any of these situations are similar or different from experiences they have had. Here are some examples of scenarios you might use.

Scenario 1

A waitress takes your $50 bill in a restaurant where your charges came to $18.50. She brings you $1.50 in change. You tell her you gave her a $50 bill, and adamantly she says that you did not. What do you do now?

This scenario will bring out culturally different ways of solving such a problem. It may bring out other stories about learners being cheated, and it will bring out opinions about why people think some get cheated. Did the waitress cheat you because she thought she could get away with it? If so, why would she think that? Or did she just make a mistake, but if that is the case, why is she arguing so adamantly that you are wrong?

Scenario 2

You have purchased a shirt on sale and, when you get it home you discover that the size is not right. When you return it to the store, you are told that because it was sale merchandise, you may not return it. The cashier tells you that it says this right on your bill. You threw your bill away when you got home. You want your money back. What can you do?

This scenario gives the group a chance to discuss common retail policies, the need to keep your bill, and to try on merchandise before purchasing it. You can teach the idea of negotiating compromises. If the store will not give you back your money, perhaps they will give you a voucher to purchase something else later, or maybe you can exchange the item then and there. If all else fails, learners can decide not to make the same mistakes twice.

Scenario 3

You live in an apartment with three storeys. The walls are fairly thin and you easily hear noise from your neighbours. One day, you hear a great commotion. A woman screams, a door slams, and then you hear someone crying loudly in the next apartment. What, if anything, do you do?

This scenario will provoke a lot of discussion and some people will adamantly say that you must not get involved, that it is not your business. Some will argue that you should knock on the door and ask your neighbour if everything is okay. Someone may suggest that you call the police. Someone else may say to wait until your husband gets home, and he can go and ask. In any case, you have here a grand opportunity to discuss spousal abuse, the laws, women's shelters, and various cultural ethics around taking responsibility for the well-being of others. In addition, various reactions among the participants may give you some clues as to which women in your class have suffered abuse and/or may still be.

K. *Give others the opportunity to be the teacher, and put yourself in the role of learner whenever the opportunity arises.* The teacher is seen as a position of power. When others feel themselves in this position and receive acknowledgement for it, they gain in confidence and in hope that they may once again feel power in their lives in their new country.

This approach is also good for teaching children. In the seventies, participatory ESL teachers in Toronto were using it with children and getting beautiful results. Children love to be given responsibility. It affirms for them that they are able and valued.

Workshop Activity

Select nine pictures of about 8½-by-11-inches in size, using old magazines and calendars as sources. Try to get a good variety—nature scenes of various sorts, different seasons, different countries, some with people, some without. Now bring together a group of five or six people—the more varied, the better. Ask them to select one or two pictures that speak to them and to share their thoughts on each. When you have finished, think about how you and the learners know one another differently as a result of this activity. Think about the language you have used to discuss the pictures. (If possible, do the exercise with an ESL class and observe how students will find the language to say what they want to say.)

The Classroom and the Community

CHAPTER 7

Accountability and Evaluation

Questions to reflect upon:

- What is the first thing you think of when you hear the word "evaluation"? How do you account for that?

- In your experience as a teacher, to what degree do you believe testing has been effective in determining the truly significant learning outcomes for individuals? For the group?

- What effect has testing, and the anticipation of being tested had on students? Is this consistent with your understanding of what is good for students?

- What other ways do you know of demonstrating accountability in programs?

Accountability and Evaluation: What Are They?

I would be surprised if many readers did not answer the first question above by saying "tests" or "testing." For a very long time, we have thought of accountability and evaluation as the same thing, at least very closely connected, and we have assumed that tests were the best way to evaluate and to demonstrate accountability. I suggest that this thinking is flawed.

Firstly, accountability and evaluation are not the same thing. Accountability is the ability to *account* for what we have done in a responsible manner; the ability to show concerned observers that we have done what we said we were going to do. Evaluation is the *means* by which we demonstrate accountability, but it is much more than that. Evaluation is, quite literally, the process of drawing value from something: *e-valu-ation*. We ask a learner, "What have you learned today?" and she says, "I understand 'co-operation' now." We ask, "Do you mean that you understand the word?" "No," she says, "I understand the *idea* of co-operation. This is good. I like it." This is evaluation. Through our questioning and her answers, we have come to understand some of the meaning and significance one learner took from an ESL program on that particular day.

The problem with tests, or rather one of the problems (for there are many), is that they measure only that which is on the test, and only then, if the learner understands how to do the test and is not distracted by other concerns such as health problems, the lovely lady sitting beside him, or worries about how he get can money to his family in the refugee camp so they can buy medicine for his sick mother.

We seldom measure what is really important; what has made a profound difference in the lives of the learners. We assume that if a learner demonstrates competence in grammar and vocabulary, he or she will find a job and be successful in the community. But that is an outrageous assumption. His or her competence, or lack thereof, is being measured against some artificial standard of correctness that we choose for the test, not by what is required by and for the particular workplace or life situation of that learner.

Nor is language the only or even the most important significator of success when one is looking for work or interacting with others in the community. I have seen many examples of people whose language and literacy skills seemed far below the mark of what was desired and even needed for the job, but whose attitude and personality were so outstanding that all else was overlooked. Many of us are beginning to include these types of *intents* in our curricula, but they are not easy to measure and so we do not bother evaluating them at all. We can and should find ways to demonstrate our success in the aspects of learning that really matter.

Guiding Questions

In working with these two concepts, accountability and evaluation, there are some initial questions to which we need answers before we begin:
- To whom are we accountable and for what?
- In whose interest do we evaluate and for what purposes?
- What type of evaluation is most effective in demonstrating that which we regard as most important in terms of outcome?
- Does the same type of evaluation serve to demonstrate accountability in terms of what is important to different stakeholders?
- Are we being accountable for the spin offs attributable to different types of evaluation such as its effect on learners, on time available for learning, on staff time, and on the stress levels of teachers and learners.

Types of Evaluation

The following types of evaluation are typically part of what can and should be happening in most ESL programs:

1. Placement Assessment

When a learner applies for an ESL program, it is important to know that this program is not only the best available program for that particular learner at that time but also that within it he or she is placed at the most appropriate level. Most programs use some sort of a screening test. In Canada, federally funded programs and many provincially funded programs have adopted a common screening tool across the country called the *Canadian Language Benchmarks Assessment*, or *CLBA*. Administered only by certified staff who have been trained in Ontario for that purpose, CLBA assessors are regularly checked to ensure that their assessments remain consistent with the standard. This standardization in assessment is a great advance from the perspective of learners in that, at last, when they are told they are Level 3 in Listening/Speaking, Level 3 in Reading, and Level 2 in Writing, that means more or less the same thing to every ESL program in the city, the province, and the country. With this assessment learners can move much more easily from one region to another and find what they are looking for (after their assessment the learners are given a card that records the date and their assessment levels). The system is not perfect, but it is a great improvement on anything that has been tried before. (The shortcomings of the *CLBA* lie in the inconsistency of post-course testing. Any organization can present their estimate of the finishing levels, but those estimates cannot be standardized because most providers are not allowed to take the training to administer the tests.)

In addition, most providers of TESL programs have testing of their own to make sure that each student is placed appropriately within a larger program. Most assessments include written testing as well as an oral interview. Interestingly, experienced teachers can generally tell within less than five minutes of an interview the level at which a student should be placed; their assessments are more accurate than the results of much longer and more stressful written tests. Nonetheless, we continue to place greater trust in numbers than we do in our own judgment. We insist on having students write tests, which may last as long as two hours, only to confirm what we knew in the first five minutes of talking to that person and looking at a writing sample. Is comprehensive testing really necessary for all placement purposes?

2. Learner Progress Evaluation

In order to determine how well the learners are progressing in the program, we frequently use tests to assess their progress. Tests are an easy-to-administer tool for assessing improvements in grammatical correctness, listening comprehension, reading comprehension, gains in vocabulary, and fluency in writing, providing that the learner does not go blank at the thought of being tested, which a few do. For educated learners, tests are an accepted way of motivating "cramming," as we used to call it. Unfortunately, and as we all know, "learning" of this sort is not necessarily retained.

One alternative we have used in an ESL literacy program is keeping *portfolios* for each learner. Portfolios are folders that include learners' work such as their compositions, exercises, and book reports. Weekly entries are dated and filed in order. In viewing a learner's portfolio over time and in an orderly manner, one cannot help but notice changes in the work: length of submissions, number and kind of corrections, changes in complexity of structures and vocabulary used, and overall fluency. Whereas it is much more time consuming to view these portfolios than to compare a handful of test scores, the portfolio system gives us much more complete and meaningful information about what a learner has and has not learned. We not only see correctness but also self-confidence and enthusiasm, both qualities which are very important to a person's ability to communicate in writing. The book reports indicate over time, changes in the type and difficulty of materials the learners have chosen to read and the degree to which they understood what they have been reading.

An alternative to tests which I found very meaningful in a workplace program were interviews I conducted with the husbands and children of workers who had volunteered (after being asked by their wife or mother) to participate in the research project. I visited ten homes of learners who had been in the classes for some time. In the presence of the learner, I asked members of their families to tell me about any changes they had experienced in their mother's behaviour which they could attribute to their mother's learning. Both the mothers and I were delighted with what they said. Teenagers were extremely happy that their mothers could now take phone messages from their friends instead of saying, "No English." Husbands were happy that their wives could now go to doctor's appointments alone or go shopping by themselves. Young children even had something to say. One young boy said that his mother did not used to go to parent-teacher meetings at school because she did not understand what was being said. But now he was proud because she came to his interview, and his teacher was happy she came. The mothers could now read letters from the children's schools and even write absence notes. Before this the children sometimes had to write the notes and their parent would sign it with an "X" or a childlike signature; the teacher would accuse the children of excusing themselves and ask for a real note.

I consider these changes in language proficiency to be very significant because the goal of our language programs is not only for the participants to speak or write correctly but also to improve the quality of their lives. When a woman feels confident enough to invite her English-speaking neighbours for dinner, she has opened a window on making new friends for herself and her family. When a learner gains sufficient confidence to ask for a raise after working for the same company for eight years and gets one, that is significant, not only in terms of his ability to support his family but also in the way he views himself and his competence in a new language. When a worker asks for and gets a promotion; when another worker stands up for his rights after being abused by another staff member; when a woman tells her doctor that she does not want to take that medicine instead of throwing it in the garbage and looking for a new doctor—these are significant changes made possible because of classroom instruction, not only in the technical aspects of the language but also in the attitudes and personality that go with the language and culture of instruction.

As an administrator, I ask teachers for both regular test scores and anecdotal reports, and I put far more stock in the anecdotal reports than I do in the test scores, which we use primarily so that learners themselves can see what they are learning. Anecdotal reports are less an evaluation of the individual learners than they are an indicator of the value of a whole program. Teachers are asked to note significant happenings in their classes that point to learning having taken place. They write such things as:

"Today, Hien asked Mohammed to please stop staring at her. She has been most uncomfortable with his stares for a long time but has said nothing. We practised making requests today and that was what she came up with, and it was REAL!"

"Mrs. Chiu came to school by bus today. She was so proud. For the last four months, her son was driving her to school, which meant that she had to arrive almost an hour before class and wait outside for half an hour until the school opened. Until now, she had been afraid to take the bus because she thought she would get lost. Now she has proven to herself that she can do it. I hope this is the beginning of her discovering more independence in her life. It is a great start!"

"Finally, Margarita went to the International Qualification Assessment Service and paid her $100 fee to get her credentials evaluated. I really believe there is no reason she cannot practise her profession here if she just jumps through the hoops. When I suggested it several months ago, she looked too discouraged to try. Now she has done it. I look forward to the results."

Learners have individual goals and individual needs and abilities. A good program enables each individual to achieve his or her own goals and maximize his or her own potential. Tests give us little indication of that—anecdotal records do.

3. Learner Progress Reports

Most programs have some sort of standardized reporting process whereby learners can know how their teachers perceive their progress at intervals during and on conclusion of a program. These reports have their pros and cons. They are good because learners know exactly where they are at in the eyes of the teacher, and where by implication, the teachers expect them to be. The reports can be bad in cases where learners are expected to show them to a husband or a social worker, who later use them to judge her negatively and put her down. It is important that teachers know exactly how reports are going to be used and by whom, and that the form they take be negotiated with learners on that basis.

Typical information on these reports includes these areas: attendance and punctuality records[1] (as these are important to employers, and learners need to understand, if they do not already, the value our society attaches to time): major test scores (if any), areas of strength and areas that need work, and suggestions for making improvements. In our programs, we did not grade learners, but we did include our estimation of finishing levels on final progress reports, as per the *CLBA* tool. These level assessments would help other providers place the learners in future educational or training programs.

Written evaluation can be followed with a one-to-one meeting between teacher and learner so that the report can be discussed. Learners often take these reports very seriously, and they can be very upset by comments they perceive to be negative. The teacher may not be aware of the extenuating circumstances that have impacted a person's progress. A personal interview gives everyone time to talk and listen without feeling they are imposing on anyone's time. These interviews are especially important for the shy student who might otherwise not yield any information about what was going on in his or her life.

Teachers at the lower levels often prefer to do oral interviews rather than preparing written reports. This is a problem only when an outside source demands documentation of progress or notification of lack of progress. Teachers can write notes for the files, but I do not like to see any notes go into someone's record that the individual has not seen. That strikes me as unfair.

Reports can be double-edged swords. An abusive husband, for example, could get his hands on a report which indicates that his wife is not making progress, which could prove dangerous to that woman. A

---

1 I have mixed feelings about these records being included in learner program reports. When someone has valid reasons for frequent absence or lateness, it just adds to their feelings of guilt and frustration to be reminded.

social worker could use a report to justify cutting someone off welfare, or not approving her continuance in another program such as job training. Such situations need to be dealt with very carefully. Our responsibility is always, I believe, first and foremost to the learner.

4. Summative Testing

Summative testing is done at the end of a program and is often used as *the* significant indicator of success or failure in learning. In that most people have good days and bad days, and some people do not respond well to testing situations, such testing is unfair to those individuals who do not "fit the mould." Like so much of our schooling, it is seen as inevitable, and it has therefore been acceptable that there will be casualties. Few policy-makers look at the cost of such "casualties" whose whole lives can be affected by the outcomes of failed tests.

If summative testing is to be used at all, let it at the very least be used in conjunction with other evaluation tools which value things which are not measurable and which evaluate the whole of a learner's journey and not just what is easily discernable at the end of the day.

5. Teacher Performance Appraisals

It is generally considered good practise to have, on an annual basis, some form of written evaluation of teaching staff. In some cases, administration lays out a form in accordance with what they value; in others, staff are invited to participate in designing a form that works for them too. In some cases, the administrator fills out the form following one or more observation from the teacher's teaching and then sits down for an interview with the teacher. In other cases, the teacher fills out one copy of the form and the administrator completes another copy. In an interview, they compare both forms, adding additional comments after a discussion of how the teacher's performance can be improved from both perspectives. Both copies of the report go into the teacher's record.

Despite their common use, teacher performance appraisals are not without problems. Both the design of an appraisal form and how it is filled out are acts of valuing what is considered to be good teaching. This process is never objective. I remember my frustration at the diametrically opposed evaluations I received in one job when there was a change of supervisor. The first supervisor had praised the way my classes seemed to flow from one topic to another with no discernable break. The second criticized that fact, saying that breaks should be very obvious to all concerned and should take place at regular time intervals. Obviously, the first and second supervisors were operating from a different set of values.

I believe it is important for us as teachers to be involved in the design and in the appraisal process itself. The purpose of teacher performance appraisals is ultimately to ensure that the quality of teaching continues to improve. For this to happen, teachers have to perceive the need and the possibility for the quality of their teaching to continue to grow. They have to feel free to admit to problems and gaps when they arise, and they have to genuinely own any decisions to change their teaching practice. If that sense of being valued and supported to grow is not there, any agreement to change is empty.

Here are some of the categories that I believe we need to include in a teacher appraisal form:

A. Relationship Between Teacher and Learners

When I am evaluating teachers, I look for a relationship of trust. I look for a learning environment of mutual respect where the learners appear to be relaxed and excited about their learning. There is laughter in the room, and there is no apparent discomfort with my presence or that of an outsider coming in to visit. (I have found that when the teacher is relaxed with visitors, the learners are. If the teacher is self-conscious, the learners pick that up immediately and start defending the teacher when it is not necessary.) I look for openness on the part of the learners, who do not hesitate to say when they do not understand, or to ask questions, or even to repeat questions where necessary. Red flags for me are authoritarian teachers, an overabundance of learners who appear afraid to speak, bored learners, and teachers who do all the talking and questioning while students do all the listening and answering.

B. Classroom Environment

The classroom should be a reasonably attractive place where learners can easily find visual aids and resources. Red flags? Empty, sterile classrooms or congested, cluttered classrooms—as without, so within. The organization and planning of the environment can be an indicator of the organization and planning of the curriculum and lessons.

C. Indications of Planning

I look for a balance of planning and reflection. I encourage flexibility when there is a reason, but I also look for a well-thought out plan as well. Lesson plans do not have to be detailed, but they should indicate what the teacher is setting out to do and include detailed notes of reflection as to what did transpire each day. I look for indications that the teacher has responded to learner input by modifying the curriculum plan.

D. Materials Chosen

Instructional materials should be correct, neatly presented, and relevant to the needs and abilities of the learner. When texts or workbooks are chosen, they should be of the highest quality, but they should, nonetheless be used critically by learner and teacher alike. The teacher should take the good but leave the bad of these resources. Red flags? Teachers who start at the beginning of a book and follow it mindlessly in order, whether or not the material is relevant or interesting. Bonus: the production of good learner-made materials for use in the classroom.

E. Activities Selected

I look for a good variety of activities. Chosen with consideration for who the learners are, their age and educational background, gender, interests, abilities, needs, and most importantly, their input! Learners should have, at the very least, choices about their activities, and at best, should feel welcome to suggest activities so that these ideas can be negotiated with the whole group.

F. Level of Learner Participation

From my perspective, in an effective class, most if not all learners will ask questions, offer suggestions, and share stories willingly with the group. I value seeing high, focused energy in the classroom. Red flag? The teacher drones on, and the students tolerate it as if they had no choice.

G. Regular Learner Evaluation of Program

In any given lesson, I expect to see some form of evaluation practised by learners. This evaluation can be formal or informal, extended or very brief, but there should be no class where learners are not given the opportunity to value what they are doing in some fashion. A very simple way of doing this is to ask learners, either at the end of a class or at the beginning of the next, what they have just learned. They need to be very specific about their learning.

H. Teacher's Comportment

I look for a teacher who looks and acts professional and who matches the environment where he or she is teaching. So, a teacher in an institution or an office building would make a bad impression on me if she showed up to work wearing jeans, shorts, tight plunging necklines, mini-skirts, or any other apparel that looked less than professional. A teacher who works in a sewing machine factory, however, might decide to wear jeans, especially if the company produces jeans. I would also look for someone who was conscious of his or her choice of words, who abided by the policies and procedures of the employing organization, and who generally acted with responsibility to the learners and to the employing organization. Red flags? Teachers who gossip behind other staff members' backs, who talk about the students when it is not necessary or appropriate, or who undermine their employer or the organization for which they work.

I. Professionalism

In addition to a teacher's behaviour, there are other aspects of professionalism, which I believe to be important. One is the teacher's on-going attention to professional development. Does the teacher show initiative in taking courses or attending workshops on her own? Does she attend those learning events that are organized by the employer after hours? Does she attend the annual conference of her professional association? Is she involved in the activities of her professional association in any way? Does she subscribe to and read a professional journal? Does she volunteer to do a workshop, or give a paper at a conference to share her ideas with colleagues? Does she advocate on behalf of the learners when those learners are unable to do so for themselves? Does she respect organizational structures? Does she show initiative in making suggestions to better the program or in spending extra time to do so? Does she exercise good judgment in making decisions? Does she demonstrate good character in her relationships with staff and students alike?

J. Attendance and Punctuality

Regular attendance and punctuality are valued in this society, and no less in classrooms that introduce learners to this society. Red flags? Teachers who miss one day a month regularly, teachers who are regularly late or just on time, or who leave the moment class is finished. These practises indicate to me that the teacher views his or her work as just a job rather than a vocation, and I would be reluctant to hire or recontract those teachers who had a track record of repeated indicators of this nature.

Good teachers often burn out by doing more than they should. I have appreciated those teachers, who rather than waiting until they are sick, have asked for leave without pay to take a much-needed holiday or who scheduled vacation time to take a much-needed break.

K. Other

We need a category to take into account those qualities that do not fit anywhere else. When a teacher sees that the resource room is disorganized and offers to stay late two nights to organize it, this gesture is much appreciated by everyone and needs to be recognized for the record. When a teacher goes the extra mile with a student who is having difficulty managing her finances, that too is very time-consuming and needs to be recognized. Or, on the other hand, if a teacher is reported to be dating a student when that is clearly against school policy, that needs to be stated as a warning in the event that similar evidence is given in the future.

There are many means of accommodating these and other values on an evaluation form. What matters most is that teachers are given acknowledgement where it is due and suggestions for improvements where that is warranted. In the event that some aspect of the teacher's work is clearly unacceptable, the expectations and time frame for meeting those expectations can be stated clearly in the annual evaluation, or, if these issues arise at some other time of the year, they should be documented in a letter to that individual.

6. Teacher Evaluation by Learners

The other means of evaluating teacher performance is, of course, to ask the learners to evaluate their instructors. Some teachers do not like this type of evaluation, but I think it is quite justified and much more relevant than any other evaluation. I have done teacher evaluation by learners as part of a program evaluation, once at mid-term and once at the end of a program. These forms are completed anonymously and turned in to some individual other than the teacher, who should never see the actual forms. The forms are tabulated, and the results returned to the teacher in that form. Problems reported in the evaluation are discussed with the teacher, who is instructed not to make any attempt to find out which student made the criticism, but simply to address it as best they can. At the same time, school policy manuals state clearly that if students are unhappy with something the teacher is doing, they should speak first to the teacher, and if that brings no results, the learners should then go to the teacher's supervisor and then to the director. It is preferable to discuss problems in the open, but students are often afraid to do this for fear that the teacher will punish them in some way. Sad but true.

7. Program Evaluation

Any program needs to be evaluated on a regular basis and changed in accordance with that evaluation. There are three groups of people who need to do this evaluation: the administration, the students, and the teachers. In addition, funders may request regular program evaluations. Here are some of the usual categories one might find on such an evaluation:

- curriculum
- materials
- activities
- teaching
- administrative support
- referral to outside agencies when necessary
- response to student requests or complaints
- facility
- support services: e.g. counselling, library, food services, audio-visual resources
- linkages with outside agencies and other educational facilities
- policies and procedures.

Obviously, formal evaluation tools would be designed differently, depending on who was to give the feedback.

The important thing about doing program evaluation regularly, is that when something is raised as an issue, everything possible be done to address it. Respondents need to know that this is the intent of the evaluation. Failure to address issues when they are raised will result in no feedback next time unless a good reason can be given as to why the issue could not be resolved to everyone's expectations.

8. Organizational Evaluation

Because most of the flaws in an organization will emerge in the program evaluation, it is not necessary to conduct an organizational evaluation every year, but it does not hurt to do it from time to time. In my experience, organizational evaluations tend to be done only when it is required (like in the case of organizations that have international or national certification of some sort, such as many settlement agencies do, or when there are some serious unsolved problems with the educational program).

My attempts to do organizational evaluation in my own organization have been less than successful, whereas my experience in doing external evaluations has been more successful. Necessary or not, staff are reluctant to criticize their supervisors when they think their job might be in some way jeopardized, even if they are encouraged to do so anonymously. They are much more likely to tell an outsider what is bothering them.

In conducting an organizational evaluation, an outsider should have access to all documents pertaining to the organization and also be encouraged to interview staff and students randomly with a variety of questions pertaining to the organization, its administration, staff, policies, and procedures. Those individuals questioned should be invited to speak freely if they have concerns or suggestions for improvement, and they should also be encouraged to give acknowledgement where due. The person or people chosen to do external evaluations should have no ties to that organization, or to any people within it; nor should there be any possibility of them being seen as having such ties. In cases where there have been a number of staff resignations, student drop-outs, or student complaints, every effort should be made to interview those individuals and make sense out of their stories.

Needless to say, an external evaluator needs great skill and integrity to gather a complete picture of what is happening, and to present a report that can be used by staff in a troubled organization to recreate a healthy one.

9. Teacher Reflections

Although seldom mandated by an employer, as a teacher I have found *teacher reflections* to be the most useful of all evaluations. By teacher reflections, I simply mean those notes that can be jotted down in five to ten minutes at the end of a class or day. When I am teaching, I write down what worked and what didn't, what I "covered" and didn't and why, how I felt about various interactions and incidents during the day, what I wanted to be sure to do tomorrow, and suggestions to myself to talk to specific individuals or to follow up on certain things. I also record those significant anecdotes so I do not forget them. Writing down my reflections makes sure that my daily experiences are not wasted, and that I learn from my mistakes and benefit from my successes. My notes help me to make sure I do not forget to do something I committed to, and that I followed up on anything that did not sit well with me during the day.

Workshop Activity

Alone, or better still with colleagues, design a performance appraisal form, which could be filled out by teachers and their supervisors to improve teacher excellence. Use the categories suggested in #5 on page 89, and add any others you feel appropriate. Choose a specific context, since a form appropriate to English in the Workplace would be different from one for an ESL classroom, in that it would have to take into account the instructor's relationship with workplace management and other workers, and, with his/her ability to cope with less than ideal teaching conditions, and his/her ability to do needs assessment.

CHAPTER 8

ESL and the World of Work

Questions to reflect upon:

- What do you think is the number one priority for most adults new to a country?
- Do you feel that our ESL programs have done enough to address those needs in past years? Why or why not?
- If you had just moved to the mythical country of Grawdjlaf and were offered a choice between taking a job for a year, which included two hours a day of language study at the workplace, or taking a four-month Grawdjlavi course and then finding a job yourself, which would you take and why? (No, you do not speak Grawdjlavi, and the actual hours of instruction add up to be the same in both options.)
- As a teacher, what knowledge do you need to prepare prospective workers for their successful participation in the labour market? What knowledge do you need to prepare actual workers to have a higher degree of control over their experiences in the workplace?

The Labour Market for Immigrants

The labour market for educated, white, English-speaking immigrants is as good as the economy allows it to be for the mainstream population. Introduce the facts of race, limited English and/or literacy skills, and/or lack of marketable job skills, and it is a whole different picture.

When you take a taxi in any large American or Canadian city, have you noticed who the taxi drivers are? Have you ever talked with them about their educational and work histories where they came from? It has been my experience that many taxi drivers are well-educated men with dark skin. Most have looked for other work before they found they could earn money driving a cab—not as much as they would earn as engineers, architects, doctors, educators, and accountants but enough to pay the rent and buy the groceries. They may speak with an accent, some mild, others heavy, and many would be more at home in an office environment than they are in a taxi cab. Many of them do what they do rather than what they want to do because they have come up against racial or other barriers in their job search, and barriers for those without appropriate work experience in the new country.

I did a poster exercise with a group of Latin American and Vietnamese women in a literacy class some time ago. I asked the learners to cut out or draw pictures of things they "liked," "did not like," and "needed," and to glue their pictures in three columns on a piece of flip chart paper. This exercise was designed to give us a means of talking about and giving vocabulary to objects with which they had some emotive relationship. When they had finished, I looked around the room and could not help but see some patterns emerge. A number of the Spanish-speaking women had cut out ads for toilet bowl cleaners and had put them in the "don't like" category. At first, I did not understand. When we began to talk about the pictures, it became very clear that the advertisements represented their night cleaning jobs, which for so many of were the only jobs they could find. These jobs paid minimum wage (or less, in some cases), and people felt badly treated by their supervisors, and looked down on by others they knew. Cleaning is another job dominated, at least in Canada, by immigrant labour.

Other typical jobs in which we find immigrants include migrant farm workers, sewing machine operators, hotel and hospital kitchen help, housekeeping and laundry staff as well as food processing and factory workers. Most workers in these jobs have limited educational backgrounds and/or poor language skills. When English in the Workplace programs are marketed in such workplaces, they may or may not be welcomed by management. If these programs are funded by a provincial government, community college, or board of education, however, they are more easily accepted. Occasionally, the employer will pay for them.

At other work sites, however, employers say quite openly, "I don't want them speaking English. Then, they won't do their work. Now is good." To these employers the immigrant labourers are seen only as tools for what they can do, not as human beings with human needs. (It could be argued that this sentiment often applies to workers in general, but in my experience, the further down the ladder one goes in terms of pay, the more the workers are exploited.) There are all too few employers who say, "Yes, these are good people, and they deserve to understand and speak the language and be able to read and write. Yes, I will pay."

In working in continuing education programs where workers come to school at night, you often hear many stories about life in the workplace, that is, if your curriculum has space for such stories to be told. Working in a menial job can be an emotionally draining experience for someone who previously worked as a professional in her or his own country. We do not realize the extent to which our identity is tied up in our work until suddenly that changes. Think of people you have known who have been laid off after years in the same job. Most tend to become very depressed until they find other work. When an immigrant has to face this change among the many others, it is not easy.

As educators, what can we do to ameliorate this reality for learners? I believe we have to find the balance between being truthful and, at the same time, being hopeful. On the one hand, I do not want to be responsible for creating unrealistic expectations in learners. On the other hand, I do not want to present my version of reality in such a way that a person feels that any effort is hopeless, for that would truly create the reality the individual fears most. Instead, I want to speak openly about the barriers I see in the labour market for people from other countries. Having done so, I want to give everything I have to support ESL learners in overcoming or circumventing those barriers.

If race is an issue, you tell it like it is and then set out to support that individual in being so friendly and diligent that one would be a fool not to hire her. If pronunciation is a barrier, you provide the individual with strategies for rewording those expressions she has difficulty in pronouncing. When religious dress such as the *hijab* (headdress worn by some Muslim women) presents a barrier, you discuss options with that individual and work with her to find an occupation and/or an employer where her manner of dress is not considered an obstacle. And, at the same time, we have to find ways of working within our communities to make people conscious of unhealthy attitudes and to be open to developing new relationships with people of all cultures and races.

Literacy can also be a barrier in the workplace. (Here I refer both to ESL literacy and to literacy for learners whose first language is English.) Increasingly, employers are expecting all employees to have good communication and literacy skills. Information is shared through printed training manuals and posted bulletins. Health and safety information is printed on MSDS sheets (Material Safety Data Sheets) and left in binders where workers are told to read them when they can. These sheets are hard for most people to read, let alone someone who is a non-reader. Even assembly-line operators are expected to write notes to the mechanics when their machines break down. Many sewing machine operators now have computers which keep track of their output and other information. No longer are there jobs that do not require literacy, for workers to be healthy and safe on the job. Even the night cleaner who used to just sweep, mop floors, and dust is now using potent chemicals which must be mixed exactly as directed if they are to be used safely. Employers are being sued if it can be shown that they did not exercise due diligence in ensuring the safety of their workers and the public, and their response is often to hire only people with Grade 12 educations or those who can pass written tests of their choice.

It is one thing to teach a literate person to read and write in another language. It is quite another to teach a person who has never learned to read and write in any language. We who are literate take our conceptual skills for granted. Only when confronted by people who lack those concepts do we realize the degree to which our lives are influenced by these abilities.

There has been much debate as to whether such ESL literacy learners should be taught literacy first in their own language or first in English since that is where they need it. That debate becomes quite irrelevant if there are no programs in place to make the choice. We can support ethnic communities in making these opportunities available within their communities, but in the meantime, we have to find ways of including basic literacy education in our ESL programs too. The ESL literacy student requires a different approach and much more time than the literate student. (For further reference, see *Teaching ESL Literacy* by Barbara Burnaby and Jill Bell.)

Employability and Job Skill Training Programs

In recent years, the straightforward ESL classroom is being supplemented or even replaced by classrooms which combine language training with job skill training and/or employability training. Work placements are often attached as well. At long last the preoccupation most immigrant adults feel for finding a self-sustaining and appropriate job has been recognized.

Employability and job skill training programs assume many forms. Employability programs include such topics as identifying skills and assets, career planning, forming long- and short-term career goals, preparing a resumé, writing cover letters, interview preparation, and basic job search strategies. These programs assume that the learner already has marketable job skills.

In the case of immigrant youth, homemakers who have married right out of high school, or refugees who sold fish from a boat, for example, marketable job skills cannot be presumed. Learners without such skills require some sort of skill training and/or certification, and preferably, an opportunity to gain experience in the local workforce by participating in work placements. (In some centres, these opportunities are called *co-op* programs because the employer and the educator are co-operating to provide training opportunities for the learner.)

The staff who work in employability and job skill training programs need different backgrounds and/or training than traditional ESL teachers. Ideally, the staff person is both an ESL instructor who can continue to work on language needs and a person with multi-faceted work experience, who understands what entry-level and new workers are going to experience in the workplace. The teacher knows the labour laws of the land and is familiar with common health and safety procedures and regulations in a variety of workplaces. He or she knows the petty power politics which govern so many interactions among workers when they themselves feel oppressed and the importance of recognizing and rising above such behaviours.

Teaching job skills/ESL is not for a person who has gone from high school to university to teaching. It is a job, ideally, for either those teachers who themselves immigrated and worked in all kinds of jobs before they got to where they are now or for those teachers who are native-born and worked a variety of different jobs before getting a teaching degree.

For me personally, the knowledge to do this work has come in two ways. As a student at university, I worked in a wide variety of entry-level jobs such as ward aide in a hospital, waitress, salesperson, and clerk. Then, when I started teaching English in the Workplace, I worked with sewing machine operators, hotel staff, hospital workers, and manufacturing and food-processing workers. These workers taught me what I needed to know about their workplaces and what it was like to be an immigrant worker. If we do not have that background personally, it is all the more important that the learners be our teachers in sharing experiences they have had in their workplaces in the new country.

English in the Workplace

In the 1980s, and somewhat less in the early 1990s, English in the Workplace (EWP) has been a popular option for teaching immigrant workers who are already employed. EWP is generally driven by the employer's desire to increase efficiency and safety on the job, and this type of ESL instruction has often been funded by governments who have recognized that it is cheaper to support someone in learning language on the job than to support him as an unemployed person on employment insurance, social assistance, or workers' compensation.

However, when the provincial and federal governments began their massive drive to get rid of outstanding deficits, workplace education programs often became a luxury, and government support was no longer there. Large employers who had vision saw that providing language training for immigrant workers as being in their interest.

These employers have recognized that commitment and dedication cannot be bought but have to be cultivated over time. By supporting the growth and development of their staff, they are attempting to meet the changing needs of the workplace of the future.

Workplace ESL programs vary considerably. These programs can be a few weeks in length or they can go on for years. They can focus exclusively on the language related to working in specific jobs, or they can combine language training with job training. For example, we recently ran a customer service program for parking attendants. The employer and program coordinator both recognized that, while the majority of employees were immigrants in need of some language support, it was not possible to separate those needs from their need to learn appropriate ways of dealing with an often difficult public on the job. Other workplace programs combine the personal and work-related language needs of the workers in planning their curriculum and materials.

As you might imagine, longer programs have a greater chance of success than the very brief ones. Our longest-running program is one with the Levi Strauss Corporation. While the majority of students study for a few years and then move on to other learning opportunities, there are a few learners who have opted to stay for the twelve years the program has run. These sewing machine operators have become literate and can communicate successfully in English. Most workers have gained confidence in taking charge of their lives at home as well as at work. The company has also seen gains in the workers' participation in workplace decision making. The employer feels the corporation would not have been able to move from piecework to wage work as smoothly as they did without the active participation of the workers in designing a system seen by all as fair.

The EWP teaching staff has become a de facto part of the plant. The instructors are invited to meetings where new concepts are being explained and to workshops where new possibilities are being explored. They use the same office facilities within the plant as the Levi staff. They are invited to Christmas parties and barbecues, wear the Levi T-shirts, and use other promotional materials with pride. Both staff and union representatives within the company make the ESL staff feel at home. Some are invited to students' weddings and anniversaries, and are there for them when they and/or their families are sick in hospital or have a baby.

The teachers feel like part of the students' lives, and hope they feel the same. Our teachers are at the plant six days a week, ten months of the year. Is this common? No, I do not believe so, but thanks to a company with vision, we have had the opportunity to see what a difference a long-term commitment can make to the workers and to the employer.

Conventions of Workplace Programs

Workplace programs have their own particular conventions chosen because they have been shown to be effective and necessary:

1. Needs assessment

Workplace education is seldom "canned" training. By that, I mean that we do not go into a workplace and deliver a pre-existent program. Rather, we work with the employer and staff to identify the specific language needs of workers and the resources available to support learning in those areas. We pull this information into a report we call a *needs assessment*. We also try to identify the power structure of an organization, not just formally but informally as well. This is very important because workers have to feel safe in their studies. They do not feel safe if they are mocked or humiliated for taking part in a program, or if their schedules are suddenly changed to make participation difficult or impossible.

While getting information is the core of a needs assessment, the teacher conducting the assessment is also building relationships within the company. His or her consideration, or lack thereof, of the supervisors' needs will determine whether those supervisors will support or sabotage the EWP program once it begins. EWP teachers need to be very conscious in cultivating that support at all times.

A needs assessment typically includes interviews with supervisors and workers, observations on the job, and a review of print materials. Sometimes, the needs assessment will include a teacher doing the job itself to see what it feels like. In preparing to do a workplace English class with busgirls and waitresses in a large hotel, I went in and worked for a day. The employer was not willing to let me work their jobs, as he felt strongly it would diminish my credibility. I worked as a hostess instead and discovered that this job involved far more than handing out menus. It was a political balancing act of noticing who had what tables, and what stage of the meal the table was at. The idea was to seat people so that all the staff had a balance in their workload—not an easy task when customers have their own ideas as to where they want to sit. Staff were angry if they did not get enough tables but were also angry if they got too many all at the same time. In addition, I was expected to help out with refilling coffee and water glasses, resetting tables, and getting the food from the kitchen to the tables when it was ready.

In the course of that one day, I learned about the stresses of working in that restaurant. I learned that in the hierarchy of the kitchen the chef has all the power and the dishwasher has absolutely none. In short, I learned many things that staff may or may not have thought to tell me, and I developed a lot of respect for everyone in that situation. I worked very hard that day, and the restaurant staff had not even expected me to use the cash register, a normal responsibility of the hostess. The needs assessment I prepared for that workplace, and the curriculum which came out of it, were much more complete for having had that work experience, which no amount of observation could have replaced. I could now "feel" the workplace.

2. Proposal

Someone has to pay for a workplace program, and no one is going to pay for an ESL workplace program unless they know two things: the anticipated outcomes, and that the EWP provider has the competence to achieve it. A well-written workplace proposal will communicate both of these points. A proposal contains the following elements:

- the needs assessment report (process and findings)
- recommended objectives/goals/intents of the program
- expected outcomes (how you will know the above have been achieved)
- time frame for program (dates for various stages of a program, frequency and duration of classes)
- resources needed
- evaluation criteria
- information about staff intended for program, if known
- budget
- expectations regarding the employer and the educator

3. Negotiated Partnership

Different providers of ESL workplace programs have different under- standings as to their role in doing workplace education and training, as do employers. The most common understanding, unfortunately, is that of the educator as *program deliverer*. In this instance, once the objectives are set, the educators come in, deliver the program, and leave. I find this interpre- tation of workplace education very unsatisfactory and unrealistic.

A good workplace program has ample contact between worker, educa- tor, and employer (managers and supervisors). The curriculum is constantly responding to changes within the work site and the environ- ment around it. I prefer to see the educator as a *change agent* working with all the stakeholders to identify and work towards the changes people see as desirable. Increased language skills are but one of those changes.

I am currently working on a project in which I provide short-term workshops for a large number of employees working in six similar hos- pital settings. While I see each worker for only thirty-two hours in the classroom, I am on the work site repeatedly over a long period. I meet regularly with the managers in most of these sites and hear their sides of the story. I see myself as having a unique opportunity to work with everyone in these situations in order to facilitate a broader understanding of several points of view. I can carry the workers' views to management and explain feelings that the workers do not feel safe explaining themselves. In turn, I can explain management policies to workers in a way that helps them to understand why some decisions have been made.

In my work I assist employees to communicate their own ideas and feelings in ways which may be more appropriate and therefore better received than in the past. By teaching in a lighthearted, humorous way, I can diffuse a lot of the fear and tension which has built up over long-standing issues. I am a change agent in these hospitals and I take this responsibility very seriously.

Not every employer (or union, in some cases) wants a change agent in an educator. They may just want a quick fix. Not every educator has the background or desire to take on all that responsibility. The secret to working successfully in ESL workplace education is to know what is called for in any given situation and what it takes to respond. We have to negotiate with the employer and/or the union the style of partnership that is most desirable in that particular situation. Included in this description of partnership is the identification of who does what. For example, it is not uncommon for workplace teachers to ask the employer to provide photocopying facilities and refreshments in situations where employees are attending classes after their work shifts. Such expectations should be made explicit up front and written into the contract; they should not be presumed.

4. Ethical Priorities

Workplace education demands a clearly identified standard of ethics. If you are an educator going into a workplace, you are going to learn a lot, often more than you ever wanted to know, about that workplace and the relationships within it. You need to be really clear about your principles in this situation. Confidentiality is a basic rule. The employer will share information you are expected not to tell the employees. The workers will confide things they do not want you to tell management. Most workplaces also expect that you will not discuss that workplace outside of that context. There may be processes or other information about the workplace that need to remain confidential to protect their profit margins. Your ability to do the job in the workplace is dependent on trust and, if you violate the rules of confidentiality, you will have no trust.

In addition, as the workplace teacher, you might well encounter situations of tension between employer and worker. You may be tempted to take sides. When you perceive injustice, your sense of justice may tempt you to side with the employees. The moment you take sides with anyone, however, you have lost your ability to work effectively in that context. Your job is to facilitate change, to enable it, not to take charge of it.

Here is a common mistake newer teachers often make in this situation. An employee complains that he is pressured to work overtime but is not paid for that overtime. Irate, the teacher goes to the employer and says that he must pay overtime to the employee. The employer swears never to have another EWP program and determines to "lay off" the employee and to get one who does not talk so much.

Is that decision right? Of course not, but what was gained by the teacher's being "right"? The employer no longer trusts not only the teacher but also the employing organization of that teacher, and even the concept of workplace education itself. Any potential benefits of enlightening the employer or empowering the workers to give voice to their own thoughts is lost for a long time. The employee has lost his job and may not even know why, and the teacher, while feeling very righteous, has also lost any possibility of working further in that company and will probably lose her employer's trust when her employer discovers what she has done.

A good workplace educator has to be very strategic. A correct response in this situation would have been for the teacher to teach the workers the law in an impartial way and ensure that the learners are conscious of the possible consequences of their actions. In provinces (and states) with good human rights and labour legislation, there is often the possibility of third-party complaints, but staff in those agencies will tell you that the consequences are often very unfavourable to the original complainants. I may have very strong feelings about what is right and what is wrong in a given situation, but as an educator, it is not my place to make decisions which will negatively impact the lives of others. It is my place to make sure that workers have the information and support they need to make whatever decisions they deem to be right for them.

In some cases, the employer may also place boundaries around what you say and do not say. One employer specifically told me that I was not to mention unions during the classes. I might otherwise have done so, but because that was a condition under which I accepted to teach the course, I was honour-bound not to do so.

In teaching teachers going into workplace programs, I have used the metaphor of walking a tightrope. I tell them that they are working for a provider, an employer, and the workers (and in some cases, the union). This is not an easy tightrope to walk. I say that if in the end you have to fall, fall with the worker, but bear in mind that you bring the rest of us down with you, and the game is over when you fall from the wire. To date, not one of our staff has, to my knowledge, "fallen." Forewarned is forearmed.

5. Final Evaluation

Any workplace project with which I have been involved has required a final evaluation at the end of each contracted period. (At Levi, we do this twice a year.) A final evaluation includes a description of the program, a copy of the curriculum which has been developed, attendance data, class numbers, and sometimes a breakdown of other interesting participant data such as jobs, gender, first language, age, etc. Samples of materials are given along with any test results or other evaluation mechanisms such as satisfaction questionnaires or summaries of interviews with supervisors. Problems are listed along with how they were resolved or what still needs to be done, and recommendations for future EWP programs are given.

A good evaluation tells the reader in a short time whether or not the program was successful, and in whose eyes, and what needs to happen next. Furthermore it is written with an awareness of who is going to read it. Corporate managers do not have a week to read a 100-page document—they want all the information presented quickly and in a crisp, easy-to-access format. In situations where educators feel the need to write a very lengthy report for their employers, it is useful to add an executive summary of no more than two pages at the front of that report.

Be sure to maintain confidentiality in preparing this report. Some information may need to be excluded or masked to protect the identity of the sources and that should be said up front. When all is said and done, the workplace educator wants to leave that workplace with the goodwill of the workers, the contact person, the supervisors and the managers, and of course, with the union as well when there is one.

In my experience, workplace education is one of the most demanding contexts for an educator. To be done successfully, workplace education requires a much larger set of skills than traditional ESL and demands of its teachers maturity, good judgment, and a willingness to work in less than ideal teaching conditions. If you ever teach in the workplace, you may teach on a cutting room floor or in a cafeteria, a discotheque, or in an office designed for one, not ten. You may have no overhead projector or black-board, your "classroom" may be noisy, and the air may be dusty. You may have several people who are not part of the classes watching and listening to you teach. You have to be very careful because your words will be repeated and often distorted. To be good at this type of work, one has to be committed to it. To learn more about EWP, I highly recommend *Teaching English in the Workplace* by Mary Ellen Belfiore and Barbara Burnaby.

Workshop Activity 1

Draw a sociogram of a workplace with which you are familiar.

A *sociogram* is a diagram where each job category or person has a symbol. These symbols are placed on the page according to your perception of the person's power. Each symbol is connected with lines and arrows according to who has influence and/or power over whom. This is not about "assigned" authority but about "real" authority, which may or may not be assigned. This exercise is not about being an artist but rather about becoming conscious about who has power. Try to do this activity with others and discuss your sociograms after you have each made one, or you may wish to do the activity as a group.

Workshop Activity 2

Plan some intended learning outcomes for one or both of the following scenarios:

A. Twenty women have been chosen from the social assistance rolls to participate in a nine-month job training program which will prepare them to work both as beginning daycare workers and as personal care attendants in extended care facilities. All but one of the women has been identified as belonging to a visible minority. Most have children but no spouse. All are physically able to work although three are emotionally upset over recent divorces and other problems. Schooling ranges from none to about Grade 6, except for one woman who has Grade 12 in India but is a long-term welfare recipient with no marketable job skills. Provision has been made to include two work placements in the nine months.

B. Twelve workers in a small garment factory have been selected for a fourteen-week workplace education program where they will be studying English six hours per week, after their shift. This factory manufactures specialty garments such as sports team jackets, work-wear for the oil industry, and pants and jackets with club logos. The workers are mostly Chinese speaking with two Spanish speakers and one Punjabi speaker. Most have very few English language skills although the Punjabi woman went to school for four years in India and was taught in English. However, she does not read and write.

Their supervisor is a very authoritarian woman who demands total obedience which she rewards with apparent, if patronizing, affection. Since their supervisor came to this country as an immigrant, she does not see why immigrants should be given language classes. In her mind, they should take responsibility for their own learning, like she did. The supevisor thinks that the workplace program will be success-ful if, at the end of fourteen weeks, the employees stop speaking their own language in the lunchroom and at least try to speak English. (You know that this is not at all realistic.) The workers are poorly paid compared with other garment workers in that city and are frequently laid off when the company does not have enough orders to fill. The company has agreed to the classes because the government is paying for them, and they are being held after working hours.

CHAPTER 9

Literacy and ESL

Questions to reflect upon:

- What is literacy?
- What level of literacy is still required in North American society?
- What is "essential" (as in essential skills)?
- What is the relationship between literacy and power in our lives?
- What is wrong with *deficit models* of literacy? (Deficit models of literacy define literacy as a lack of sufficient skill in reading and/or writing.)
- In whose interests do we read and write?

Meanings of Literacy

The questions above are not at all easy to answer. There are no simple answers; that is why it is important to be thinking about what these questions mean in different contexts, to different people. Simplistic understandings only serve to weaken our educational practices. The dictionary definitions are very straightforward. *The Canadian Oxford Dictionary* (1998) defines literacy as (1) the ability to read and write, and (2) competence in some field of knowledge, technology, etc. (e.g., computer literacy). Until recently, we would not have seen the last definition of literacy, but since the advent of computers where many of us who had formerly considered ourselves highly literate suddenly felt like small children, we are increasingly seeing the need to define different literacies. The second definition is a good place to start as it places literacy in the context of what is required by society.

Those of us who go to graduate school after years of being out of school recognize an academic literacy that we have to get back into. When we work in workplaces that specialize in any one of a number of technologies, we realize the need to become literate in the vocabulary and systems of that technology. These are functional literacies. All of us have to discover which ones apply to us, as do the ESL learners who come to our country, recognizing that, for some of these learners, there is no foundational literacy to build on. There are also many, many changes to what they have known because the world in which we live may be very different from the one they came from.

Beyond functional literacies, however, we need to consider the social construction of literacy and the meanings attached to literacy, and hence to illiteracy, in our societies. Starting with the latter, Pierre Bourdieu used the term *cultural capital* to talk about the knowledge which gives us power in communication with others. A personal experience of many years ago gives me a lived understanding of this term.

I was substitute teaching in a rural Grade 6 classroom. I was just beginning to gain the trust of these young people when one of them ran into the classroom at the same time the bell rang, excitedly telling us that he had gotten a "shutout" the night before. He looked at me with great pride! Being a person not inclined to spectator sports and feeling quite displaced in rural Alberta, I had not the slightest idea what he was talking about. When I asked him what a shutout was, I got a look of sheer incredulity and then disgust. He turned his back on me and muttered to the class, "She don't even know what a shutout is." (A shutout is when a goaltender prevents the opposite team from scoring during the entire game.) Any credibility I could have had with this group was gone because I did not know their world, and my ignorance of this simple hockey term gave me away. How could they ever trust that I would understand them after that? My ignorance had cost me power in this situation. I lacked the necessary cultural capital.

Much of our cultural capital comes to us from print. From reading the newspaper, we are able to intelligently discuss the affairs of the day with our colleagues and neighbours. From books, we stay current on good literature and social analysis. Whereas much of our dependence on print has been replaced by television and movies, it is still considered an asset to be well-read and to know what is going on in the world around us. Those who cannot enter into the conversations of their peers are deemed to be ignorant and are judged accordingly. Different literacies accord us different kinds of respect depending on where we are and with whom we relate. Respect gives a person influence, which is one form of power.

And so we see three different ways of looking at literacy. 1) Schools look at literacy in an absolute sense and record grade scores that are interpreted as a measure of worth in accessing further study and in finding employment. 2) The many functional literacies describe our ability to use print in particular settings as prescribed by others who want us to have those skills. 3) The literacies of power take us one more step and describe the ability to use print to act on our world—to make a difference.

Rhetoric is the power of persuasion exercised either verbally or in writing. Rhetoric used to be a skill taught in schools. Now, many people do not know what the term means. We expect our leaders to have rhetoric and, indeed, a true leader is one who has the power to persuade people of the value of a particular direction and to mobilize them to move in that direction. We live in a society where change comes when leadership is exercised. We write letters to the editor, to our politicians. Briefs, reports, and position papers are tools used to challenge the status quo. Books which hit the best-seller lists are enormously powerful tools in the shaping of social consciousness. Yet how often do we see books written by the poor, by refugees, by the uneducated? Not often, and when it happens, it is often because someone not in that state has collaborated with a professional author to tell that person's story. Recently Rudy Wiebe collaborated with Yvonne Johnson, a First Nations woman currently serving a term for first degree murder, to write *Stolen Life: A Journey of a Cree Woman*.[1] Johnson had a story to tell and was wise enough to know that her chances of telling it alone were minimal at that time.

In the teaching of literacy, we need to recognize all the literacies as they apply to a particular learner or learners. If a person needs a particular score on some test in order to achieve his/her other goals, then we have to be concerned with absolutes as measured by that test. If a mother wants to read stories to her children to give them a good head start at school, that functional skill is where we focus our energies, at least to begin with. If a group of learners suffers because they lack power over their experiences, then it is the naming of their world and the identification of their issues which forms the core of the teaching-learning experience.

Several authors in both literacy and ESL literacy have written about the social construction of literacy. Jenny Horsman[2] recalls media descriptions of people who are illiterate as "chained in prison," "disabled," "caged and blind." She goes on to say that the women thus described are being shortchanged, and that our focus on their perceived deficit is causing us to miss the really important issues in their lives, issues such as violence. We see neither their joys nor their successes nor do we recognize the barriers which prevent many learners from realizing their potential. Literacy programs offer them the promise of success, not taking into account the possibility that success may be defined by jobs not even available to those who do become literate.

In such instances, Horsman suggests, the offering of a literacy program may serve the interests of the social worker who is trying to get the learners off assistance but may simply further depress the women who, after having passed their course, are in the same situation they were before all their hard work. Who defines what is considered to be necessary literacy and how it is to be achieved? Seldom are such definitions composed by those who study in the programs designed to teach literacy.

An American study on adult ESL literacy done by Heide Spruck Wrigley found that, whereas there are many types of ESL literacy programs available throughout the United States, "the types of literacy stressed often depend less on the greatest need in the community than on the availability of funding."[3] In Canada, too, we see that the National Literacy Secretariat, while able to fund many types of activities for native-speaker literacy, is not able to fund activities for ESL literacy. They take the position that ESL literacy is the responsibility of the Immigration Department. Instead of attending to the needs of our citizens, we get caught up in the politics of who is responsible for what. Community literacy activists have been forced to develop the skills of wording their proposals, not to reflect the best interests of the prospective learners, but in the way which will get their proposals approved.

Issues In ESL Literacy

1. What Is ESL Literacy and Who Is It For?

When we talk about ESL literacy, we are usually referring to those learners who were not given access to formal education in their first language and hence did not become literate in that language. However, we may also mean those learners with very limited education who have the beginnings of literacy skill but lack enough to serve their needs as workers and citizens. Or, we may include those who are literate in a language with a very different writing system, such as Arabic, Chinese, or Punjabi, for example. Most people feel somewhat lost in dealing with ESL literacy learners because they lack the spoken language on which to begin to build reading and writing skills. In addition, most ESL programs presume the learner's ability to read and write. ESL literacy is a no man's land in ESL, and it is one with which even the most experienced instructors still struggle.

While we need to attend to these learners, many argue that ESL literacy has to be viewed in a larger context in terms not only of the skills that all ESL learners need to function successfully in the world around them but also in terms of the relationship between literacy and power. Such educators argue for participatory approaches to ESL, in which all learners have the opportunity to name their experiences here and set their own learning goals.

2. Access

Access is a huge issue in ESL literacy. ESL, when funded by governments, is often apportioned out in parcels of time, which are the same for everyone, regardless of ability. It may be a set amount of time, or it may be a time that ends when learners attain a certain level of skill, assuming that skill can be assessed accurately and that it is in the interests of those doing the assessing to do so, both of which are questionable assumptions. Seldom is a learner looked at as an individual and given time to learn what he or she needs to learn according to their abilities, their job skills and experiences, and their goals in this society. One bright individual who has already studied English in her own country and needs only the opportunity to develop an ear for the language here may do very well with four months of study while another individual who has never been to school before might need a year before he has really developed enough spoken skill to work safely in even an entry-level job.

In addition, literacy has been too often associated with volunteers rather than qualified instructors. Because literacy takes time, governments too often have not been willing to commit the funds to offer solid programs which would enable learners to develop their knowledge and skills relatively quickly by allowing them to study full-time.

Workplace education is one good solution to the need for ESL literacy but this depends on employers or unions who see value in the program either for the workplace or for the individual workers. Some employers do see the benefits of providing learning opportunities on-site and/or giving paid time to workers to attend such programs off-site. One barrier that presents itself when this option is chosen is the shift barrier. Many workers in need of such skills are shift workers, and it is a nightmare to plan programs when workers are spread over two or three shifts, especially if they are working in seven-day-a-week jobs where everyone has different days off, and those days off change. Workers in hospitals and extended care facilities, for example, often have these schedules.

What it would take to eliminate the access barrier would be a government funding body sufficiently committed to a literate society that they would dedicate both the funds and the time to provide a variety of programs for learners, as long as they need them. It would also take employers who were aware enough to see that a literate workforce is a safe, committed workforce able to adapt to the changing needs of the future. And it would take learners who believe that it is in their interest to continue learning over their lifetimes.

3. Cross-Cultural Issues

Learners learn much more from being in the classroom than simply the subject of instruction—in this case the English language and/or literacy. They are also absorbing the new cultural values and ways of being of the new country. We sometimes forget that learning itself has cultural aspects to it. For example, learners from traditional educational systems may expect the teacher to behave in very authoritarian ways and may interpret the teacher's invitation to participate fully as coming from someone who does not know what she is doing or someone who is disorganized. Such learners expect the teacher to determine the curriculum and deliver the goods. One of the things I have loved about ESL literacy is that learners seldom have such expectations because they have little or no experience in classrooms of any kind and are open to anything that is interesting.

Gender can be a cross-cultural issue too. Some Muslem men, for example, cannot accept being taught by a woman. Or, the cultural behaviours expected of men and women in the classroom may be different. McGroarty[4] describes an anxious student who was uncomfortable with the circular arrangement of desks, believing that such a set-up was conducive to other men looking at his wife, which he deemed to be unacceptable. Gender may even be an obstacle to literacy learning itself in situations where a husband feels quite strongly that a literate wife means an independent wife, and he does not want an independent wife.

Cultures have their own taboo topics. In our society, one does not typically ask a woman how old she is (especially if she is over forty) or how much she weighs. In another society, one might not talk about death. Whereas one student might love to bring pictures of his family to share with the class in a writing exercise, for another student, that topic could bring up too painful memories of lost relatives. Some learners would love to talk about politics and religion, seeing it as an opportunity to convince others of their beliefs, while some would see such topics as out of place in the classroom.

4. Learning Styles

Just as learners have different cultural expectations of the classroom and the teacher, so they pose a variety of learning styles. In a recent workshop, I was reminded of this when a Native (First Nations) participant in the workshop said nothing unless I asked her a question. Mostly, she looked down at her table and sat quietly, and I jumped to the unfortunate conclusion that she was bored with the workshop. How surprised I was at the conclusion of our time when she quietly waited until everyone else had left and then came forward with a gift, a card, and a heartfelt statement of all she had learned in the three days we had together. She had learned by watching and listening, carefully attending to everything that was going on. I learn by asking a lot of questions and testing out my conclusions verbally, and I had made the mistake of forgetting that this is not how everyone learns.

Some of us are visual learners while others are auditory or kinesthetic. Some of us are very orderly and concrete in our learning styles while others are random and abstract. As educators we need to present a variety of learning opportunities to ensure that everyone finds something which accommodates their own styles of learning.

5. Learning Disabilities

One of the greatest frustrations in ESL and ESL literacy classes results from the presence of students with learning disabilities. Because many of us know little about learning disabilities to begin with, and because learners already present limited knowledge and skill in the language, we often fail to recognize disabilities when they are there. Most communities have no means of testing such learners in their first languages, and we do not know how to enable such learners to learn when they do not respond as expected to the ways we have learned to teach.

It seems to me we have three choices when confronted with this reality. We can ignore it, which sadly many do. We can become technically more proficient on learning disabilities by taking special education courses, then hopefully we will recognize such learning problems more easily when we are confronted with them. Or (and I realize many readers will think I am a little bizarre here) we can let go of our logic and listen to our intuition in working with such learners.

For me, logic always has shortcomings because it is dependent on what I know—or rather what knowledge I have acquired. I never know enough. Intuition, on the other hand, presents itself as wholesale knowings without explanations. How do you know?—you just do! My intuition kicks in when I stop trying to figure someone out and simply try to be present to that one person, to appreciate the fullness of his or her humanity, and to enjoy him or her as a person. Then, I say or do whatever I am moved to do and, lo and behold, it is often just right.

Intuition does not work if I am feeling threatened, so in situations where I feel incompetent, for example, I first have to deal with my own issues and only then can I be free to open myself to knowing the other person and providing what is needed at that moment. (I recognize that this advice may be inappropriate and even dangerous to the person who has not recognized and/or developed her intuition as a trustworthy way of knowing, and I hope that if this advice does not suit you, you will ignore it. However, to leave it out would be dishonest because this is genuinely how I deal with some situations which would otherwise be beyond my reach.)

6. Support

According to Fingeret,[5] learners learn much better when they are part of a solid community of their own culture. When this is present, they have someone to go to when they are lonely; they have activities which re-situate them in the cultural ways of daily life they may have left behind. They have established relationships of trust and respect to support them in resolving the challenges they face in their new lives.

An issue in many communities is whether or not literacy should be first taught in the first language. While that makes a lot of sense from an ideal perspective, it does not make sense to learners whose daily life is in English; learners who would prefer to use their valuable time to learn the skills they need in that language. Why, one Laotain woman asks, would she want to become literate in Lao when there is nothing to read in that language and no one to write to because her family is also illiterate. She wants a better job in Canada, and for that she needs English literacy.

7. Methodology

Even as ESL and literacy each have a multitude of approaches to instruction, so does ESL literacy. One way of looking at this variety would be to imagine a continuum with phonics at one end and the investigation of Freire's *generative themes* at the other.[6] Many volunteers without a teaching background appreciate the simplicity of the Laubach materials, which build around the development of a phonics reading system. This is a technically designed approach to reading.

Freire, on the other hand, has a highly politicized view of literacy and its place in the lives of the learners, and his methodology begins by getting down to the real issues in people's lives. Between these two approaches are several other terms you may have heard: *whole language*, LEA (Language Experience Approach),[7] the *Learner-Centred Approach* and the *Participatory Approaches*, which are often known as Freirian approaches. All of these approaches come to us from different directions, and they occasionally overlap. In reality, most experienced instructors use an eclectic mix of methodologies in any case, doing whatever works in a given situation.

Whole language, an approach advocated by Ken Goodman and widely used in the public school system, is noted for its determination to teach reading in whole contexts rather than decontextualizing this process and breaking it down into its component pieces. Whole language is based on functional understandings of reading and writing development and uses a selection of materials taken from real contexts: reading signs and menus, writing letters and stories, and reading instructions. Portfolios replace tests as a means of assessing reading and writing development.

Whereas traditional curricula are prepared ahead of time, learner-centred[8] curricula are negotiated with the learners and are flexible and open to change at any time. This approach goes a little further than whole language in that language learning is recognized as a collaborative effort between learners and teacher, and depends on ongoing dialogue to ensure the continued relevance of what is being learned.

The participatory approach goes one step further than the learner-centred approach in that its objectives are for social change. It is a means of personal and social transformation. Authors such as Auerbach,[9] Fingeret, and Barndt[10] have written about the applications of participatory education in literacy and ESL.

8. Assessment

Assessment is a big issue in the literacy field because funders think assessment means testing and see testing as the only way to determine accountability in the expenditure of public funds. In fact, there are different types of assessment which are important. There is the *needs assessment* which is done to determine initial learning priorities. There is the *placement assessment* that enables the educator to determine at what level a learner should be placed within a learning program. And there is *ongoing assessment* which ensures that learning is taking place.

Auerbach shares a lovely insight into the word itself. The word "assess" comes from the Latin "assidere" which means to sit beside. Participatory educators "sit" beside the learner and discuss his or her background, preferences, goals, and ways of learning. They attempt to immerse themselves in the learners' lives in order to see something of their perspective on the world, and they learn to respect those perspectives.

Whereas delivery-based programs measure student progress at the end of a course, participatory programs use ongoing assessment tools which are as much for the learners as they are for the teacher. Learner portfolios, for example, can be added to each week enabling anyone who is interested to see where a learner started, what he or she has been doing, and where he or she is now. Sitting down with someone's portfolio will help you to see interests, developing strengths, and areas that still need work. Most of all, perhaps, the portfolio enables the learner to recognize the progress being made over time and feel proud of that.

Other assessment tools[11] which can be used in ESL literary programs include surveys, learner-compiled inventories of language and literacy use, interviews, and a review of selected reading materials. Class discussions and dialogue journals are other tools for gaining insight into what is needed.

9. Politics of Literacy Funding

We have already mentioned some of the funding difficulties that face would-be literacy programmers. There are other politics involved, some of them between providers themselves.

When providers are set up by funders to compete both for scarce funding and for students in a marketplace that has too many programs, one strategy they often use is to market themselves as being all things to all people. So we see universities offering not only high-level instruction for academic purposes but also literacy for refugees. We see settlement agencies doing not only settlement language classes but also offering TOEFL preparation and classes for engineers. When I see one organization that claims to do everything equally well, I am automatically suspicious. Yes, it is possible, but highly unlikely.

Organizations develop around their histories of need and the abilities and passions of particular staff people. An organization sensitive to the needs of illiterate refugee women is seldom as good at doing university preparation, and conversely an organization with the skills to do a good job of university preparation is seldom proficient at meeting the needs of literary learners.

Providers need to have faith that if they do what they do well and let others do likewise, they will best serve both their interests and those of the learners. No one can do it all nor should they try.

Literacy Skills

Whatever our approach to literacy, we have to recognize that there is a need in the community for a great variety of functional skills in literacy. Learners need to learn more than to read and write stories. They need to be able to read bus schedules, directions for using appliances, maps, instructions for workplace procedures, MSDS (Material Safety Data Sheets), tables, graphs, and possibly stock market reports, to list but a few. Too often we assume that learners will automatically transfer the literacy skills from narrative over to other forms of documents, but that is not so. Many teachers, including me, struggle with printed directions for putting things together or with computer manuals. Literacy must be contextualized into the lives of the learners; instruction is effective when it is situated firmly in that reality.

Workshop Activity I

Imagine that you are going to meet a group of fifteen men and women who want to improve their literacy in English. All have intermediate level speaking and listening skills, but they have a wide variety of reading and writing skills. Prepare two tables with materials that they can use as an inventory the first night of class. One table will be for reading materials learners might use in their daily lives, and the other table will be for possible writing tasks. Find as many materials as you can which may be suitable. Some materials would be from the home (utility bills, flyers, instruction manuals, recipes, etc.). Others would be from work (applications, cheque stubs, bulletins, collective agreements, etc.). Still others might be from the community (signs, newspapers, driver's manual, etc.) The idea is to have them choose the five learning materials or tasks on each table that they most want to learn and/or work with, and also point out those reading materials and tasks that they feel confident in already. If you can do this activity with someone, so much the better. You may wish to match these found materials to the descriptors in the Canadian Language Benchmarks document to attach levels to them.

For Further Reading

Bell, J. and B. Burnaby. 1984. *A Handbook for ESL Literacy*. Toronto: OISE Press in association with Hodder & Stoughton Limited.

This is still the classic Canadian text for teaching ESL literacy. The authors cover who the students are likely to be and how to teach the various aspects of literacy: pre-literacy, reading, writing, multi-level classes. A very practical resource for anyone new to this area.

CCLOW (Canadian Congress for Learning Opportunities for Women) 1996. *Making Connections: Literacy and EAL Curriculum from a Feminist Perspective*. Toronto: CCLOW.

This book is the result of a lengthy and fascinating process of collaboration among a group of women who spanned the country looking for projects and ways of understanding education that respected women; in particular, women learning literacy. The voices in the book are diverse but complementary in their exploration of such topics as literacy and identity, literacy and self-esteem, and more.

Endnotes

1. Rudy, Wiebe (with Yvonne Johnson). 1989. *A Stolen Life: A Journey of a Cree Woman* Toronto: A.A. Knoft Canada.
2. "The Problem of Illiteracy and the Promise of Literacy" 1994. In *Worlds of Literacy*, Hamilton et al, Ed., Clevedon: Multilingual Matters Ltd. and Toronto: OISE.
3. Heide Spruck Wrigley "Adult ESL Literacy: Findings from a National Study," ERIC Digest, National Clearinghouse on Literacy Education. Sept. 1993.
4. Mary McGroarty. 1993. "Cross-Cultural Issues in Adult ESL Literacy," ERIC Digest. National Clearinghouse on Literary Education.
5. A. Fingeret. 1983. "Social Network: A new perspective on independence and illiterate adults." *Adult Education Quarterly*, 33(3), 133-146.
6. Paulo Freire. 1968. *Pedagogy of the Oppressed*. New York: Seabury Press.

7. The Language Experience Approach is used frequently in teaching literacy to a native speaker as it builds on the oral skills the learner has in the language. The person instructing would take the speaker's stories as is and use them to develop literacy, without worrying about whether or not the grammar was standard.

8. I do not know any teacher who does not consider his/her classroom to be learner-centered. I have put quotations around this term here to indicate that this is a term used in the literature to describe a particular approach.

9. Elsa Auerbach. 1992. *Making Meaning, Making Change: Participatory Curriculum Development for Adult ESL Literacy*. McHenry, IL and Washington, DC: Delta Systems and Center for Applied Linguistics.

10. Deborah Barndt et al. 1982. *Getting There: Producing Photostories with Immigrant Women*. Toronto: Between the Lines.

11. Kathleen Santopietro Weddel and Carol Van Duzer. 1997. "Needs Assessment for Adult ESL Learners." ERIC Digest, National Clearinghouse on Literacy Education.

CHAPTER 10

Race and Ethnicity in the ESL Classroom

Questions to reflect upon:

- How serious a problem is racism where you live? How do you know?
- What experiences have you had with people of other races, and to what extent have you judged those experiences to be positive and/or negative?
- How do issues of racism present themselves in your classrooms?
- How have you worked with issues of racism in the past?
- How can you work with those issues in the future in order to ensure the strongest and best possible outcomes for all concerned?

Background

Race is a problematic notion. *The Canadian Oxford Dictionary* defines race as (1) Each of the major divisions of humankind, each having distinct physical characteristics, and (2) A tribe, nation, etc., regarded as of a distinct ethnic stock. *Racism* is defined as "prejudice or antagonism based on one's perceptions of race in another." Rather than get into the obvious difficulties this whole notion poses, especially when we try to label races, this chapter discusses the issue of racism from the perspective of the ESL teacher.

The major focus is around skin colour as a means of discerning difference, but we must remember that it is not skin colour alone which leads to racial discrimination. Racism can also be based on any characteristic which makes one person or group stand out as different in relation to another person or group. It might even be the language a person speaks or the accent with which that person speaks English, regardless of how he or she looks. It might even be the person's last name, as has been the case in some occasions of discrimination against Jewish people.

Race as a Social Construct

The UNESCO Statement of Race and Racial Prejudice, as quoted in the *International Social Science Journal* (Vol. 20, No. 1 1968): 93-97, outlines the nature of racism as a social construct:

> The human problems arising from so-called "race" relations are social in origin rather than biological. A basic problem is racism, namely, anti-social beliefs and acts which are based on the fallacy that discriminatory inter-group relations are justifiable on biological grounds.

Berdichewsky, in his book *Racism, Ethnicity, and Multiculturalism,* struggles with the artificial nature of the race construct saying that it "acts as an ideological tool to perpetuate the concept of race, and therefore racism." Social scientists are more comfortable using terms such as *ethnic group* to describe groups with distinct social traits. The author goes on to say that race was not used to differentiate people by skin colour until after World War II. That being the case, we can see race as an historical construct. Ethnicity is a more viable concept for use in Canada in that it defines a community by its social, economic, and cultural factors.

As a white, middle-class teacher raised in a small, mostly white community, I have had very different experiences from those of you raised in large cities where the presence of people of colour has drawn attention to the issues of race and ethnicity in those communities. Like many teachers, for years I thought that the answer to this problem in the classroom was simply to ensure that I was fair and others were also fair in their dealings with all people. That all changed when I began to work closely with a woman who is Black. It changed for two basic reasons. The first was that she was constantly drawing my attention to issues to ensure that I did not miss them, and the second was that just being with her ensured that I experienced more racial issues than I had.

Spending a lot of time with this woman, as we had become friends as well as colleagues, taught me a great deal and raised a lot of questions. What I used to think of as unfortunate coincidences now seemed more than that. When the two of us registered together, in the same envelope, for a conference, my registration was received and hers was mysteriously lost. A coincidence? Probably, but when one begins to experience an inordinate number of such coincidences, one after the other, it is difficult to maintain that level of tolerance.

Our experiences in Canada were very different from our experiences in the United States. When we traveled to conferences in Canada, we felt like equals and were treated as such. Race was seldom an issue, although when it was, it really was. When we traveled to conferences in the United States, she felt acknowledged and included for her blackness, and I felt separated and excluded; the Black community in the United States has a way of being very present to its own. While I understand where that has come from, I nonetheless found it very disconcerting to be excluded.

While race may not have been an apparent issue at most local and regional conferences of our peers, it was frequently an issue elsewhere in our own province. When we went to a small town to do a workshop and arrived an hour early, we decided to get a coffee in the local McDonalds. This was a white community, and our presence in the restaurant seemed to paralyze everyone. It was the coldest, most uncomfortable feeling I have had for a long time, and when my friend noticed my reaction, she urged me to ignore it and said she had that experience all the time. I found it difficult to know how one could retain such a healthy self-esteem in the face of such cold exclusion.

On another occasion, we were sitting in a coffee shop in Calgary following a provincial conference when an incident occurred that enabled me to see clearly how racism is taught and learned with no conscious intent. A woman had come in with her two children and sat in the booth next to us. A few minutes later, her husband and two male friends joined them. As there was no room in the booth, the woman suggested to the two friends that they share the booth across from them. One laughed and asked why she was "treating him like a Black man". They all laughed. I was struck dumb. I could not believe he had said that. I could hardly breathe, so conscious was I of how painful I assumed this must be for my friend. She, however, appeared unperturbed although mildly annoyed when I said I had never heard that expression before. She heard it all the time and related a story of how her brother had heard the expression used at a meeting he attended only the week prior. She could not believe I had never heard anyone say that before, but I hadn't.

Now, I ask myself, was it that I had never heard this expression before or that it had never registered before? I know I am not conscious of ever having heard it, but if she has heard it so often, I have to wonder why I have not. It was an offensive but highly revealing remark indicative of the omnipresence of racism in our society. Our first task as educators is to acknowledge the insidious presence of racism and confront it wherever we find it.

The English Language

Believe it or not, the English language itself is filled with traces of racism. First, there are the childhood legacies that those of us in our fifties will remember from our younger years. As embarrassed as I am to recall this, we used to buy "nigger toes" at Christmas time (Brazil nuts) and "nigger babies" at the candy store (black jujubes). We knew the story of Little Black Sambo and frequently said, "Eenie, meanie, miney, mo. Catch a nigger by the toe. If he hollers, let him go. Eenie, meanie, miney, mo." I am happy to say this is not part of my children's legacy, but as a child I knew of no Black people in our community, and I never had cause to realize that what I was doing and saying was so terrible. Happily, these blatant insults have been more or less eliminated clean, and most of the children I know today have never heard them. These expressions are, nonetheless, back there in our memories doing who knows what damage to our understandings. We need to be mindful of what they are doing to our perceptions.

There are other racist words, expressions, and constructs that are still very much part of the english language today. Take all the metaphors around black and white. We have the Black Knight and the White Knight, or a black day in history. Those who would pretend that racism is not a big issue in our society may argue that these metaphors have to do with Light and Darkness, not with race. Nonetheless, when we connote black with Evil and white with Good as words, we have another force playing around with our subconscious. What are the effects of this kind of language? What about words like "denigrate" which are so hidden in their root meanings (to put down, to treat like a "nigger") that we do not even think about their origins when we use them?

Perhaps even more insidious are the constructs within the grammar itself. Just as women wrestle with the absence of an inclusive pronoun in English and the awkward renderings we use in its place, so do people of colour when they consciously wrestle with the racist features of English. It is not only Black people who face racism; it is potentially all people who are perceived as being different, and therefore threatening, by another ethnic group due to features attributed to race.

People of colour are frequently victimized. It was a Japanese international student who pointed out to me the hidden bias of the adjective endings of words indicating countries. "Why," he asked, "do we say English, French, and German but Chinese, Japanese and Vietnamese, for example?" When he first asked me this, I argued that it must be the vowel-consonant structure of the words themselves which yielded these endings, and I failed to see that there was any racial slur inherent to these spellings. He argued that when these adjectives came into the language, not that long ago as languages go, the English-speaking world was in a colonial relationship with these parts of the world and that "-ese" was given as an indicator of inferior status. I still had my doubts.

What changed my mind was his next question, "Why, then, do you know that when you are making up a noun to describe something you do not like, you instinctively add "-ese" to make the verb?" His example was "bureaucratese" to describe the red tape we all hate in dealing with governments. The moment he said this, I knew he was right and I was horrified.

How can we eradicate racial bias from our consciousness when it is embedded in the very language we use to communicate? My answer to that is that we must change the language, whatever that takes, and that can only be done with great difficulty, and only if we accept that there is racism and it is deadly in its destructive ability.

History

I have only respect for the Black and White men and women of the large American cities who manage to have genuine friendships across racial divides because when I see the pressures acting against that possibility in my own experiences, I can only admire the men and women with the vision and fortitude to overcome those barriers. In many parts of Canada, interracial friendships may not be as difficult to make or maintain because racism is neither so overt nor widespread and because our society at least places a verbal priority on diversity. However, it is still difficult to have a close relationship with a person whose history and experiences are vastly different from our own because understanding is difficult in such circumstances. Inasmuch as we want those close to us to understand us, they can only understand what we enable them to understand and then only if both parties are committed to trying to do so.

There is a history of racism that will not go away with good intentions. Slavery was present in Canada and the United States, a fact of which some Canadians are unaware. If you visit Halifax, be sure to take time to go out to the Black Cultural Centre in Dartmouth. There you will have a good introduction to the history of the Black community in Canada, its achievements, and its pain.

And it is not only the Black community that has suffered the injustices of racism. In Canada, look at the experiences of people of Chinese origins early in our history. Many Chinese workers lost their lives in the building of the national railway, for example. Look at what happened to the Japanese-Canadians during World War II. They lost everything. Men and women with educations and good jobs were sent to work in the interior of British Columiba or in the beet fields of southern Alberta, children and grandparents working side by side.

And lest we think that is all behind us, is it really? When you go to a large hotel, take a look at the guests and the people cleaning your rooms. Are the racial proportions the same as those of the community in which that hotel is located or are they different? In my experience, it is often people of colour who are working as cleaners in hotels. In

Canada, it is the Asians and people from the Indian sub-continent. In the eastern United States, it is often African-Americans. Who drives our taxicabs? In Edmonton, there are many cab drivers with dark skin who have come from the Middle-East and Africa. Many of these men are very well-educated but were not able to find professional jobs here, even though they are fluent in the language.

Manifestations of Racism in our Societies

Two types of racism are generally recognized: the individual personal racism that is so unpleasant and uncomfortable, and the institutional or *systemic racism* which is so much further reaching. Both are destructive, but individual acts of racism may be argued and battled in human rights courts whereas systemic racism is much broader, better disguised, and infinitely more difficult to overcome, as it has the weight of an entire social structure behind it.

The authors of *The Colour of Democracy* use the term *democratic racism* to describe those biases and social practices that are so widespread, they are seldom questioned:

- The acknowledgement of some voices and the ignoring of others.
- The Eurocentric bias in education at all levels.
- The media focus on social problems within the Black and Vietnamese communities—the public comes to associate these groups with crime.
- Policing based on a "we-they" mentality.
- Brushing aside or trivializing allegations of racism.

A 1993 University of Toronto study on "Employment Equity in the Workforce" shows clearly the gender and race imbalance of student and faculty at the university by providing the following statistics.

	Men	Women	Visible Minorities
Faculty	76.2%	23.8%	9.5%
Students	40.9%	59.1%	38.7%

These figures leave no doubt in our minds that something has prevented the natural distribution of work in accordance with the proportion of the populations in these three categories.

For other examples of systemic racism, we can turn to all of our social institutions: schools, the legal and justice systems, governments, and so on. The first problem is denial. A letter to the *Edmonton Journal* from a parent shows us how prevalent such denial is:

Ten years ago, I was a concerned parent of minority children attending Harry Ainlay High School; there were confrontations between ethnic groups and the response from the principal was, "No problem here—you are overreacting."

The first time I heard the word "nigger" used on a playground was here in Edmonton. Having both children of colour and white children I was acutely aware of the subtle and overt forms of racism in our community. We do not fight these ignorant responses and fears by pretending they do not exist. They are every bit as strong as in the US or South Africa, expressed less openly.

I do not blame the schools for doing nothing. They simply reflect parents' wishes. When communities speak up and say we will no longer tolerate confrontations along racial lines and do something constructive, then perhaps teachers and administrators in co-operation with communities will first inform themselves so they can in turn fight the values and intolerance that ignorance and apathy breed. Then perhaps teachers will feel free to speak out and sign their names. (*Edmonton Journal*, 1996, July, p. A7.)

I have heard similar denials, one from a teacher in the above-mentioned school who asked her high school students about racism as follows: "There is no racism in this school, is there?" (inflection down on the last word). To be sure, no one contradicted her, but they had a lot to say after class was dismissed.

One of the most difficult challenges faced by conscious teachers in the school system is to recognize those aspects of the system which automatically favour one group of learners over another, such as teaching-learning styles and tests, for example. The Native woman to whom I referred in the previous chapter reminded me of how Native people have learned in their cultures for centuries. She was listening to what everyone said and weighing it all against her own experience. Historically, Native people learned in nature, where one quietly watched and listened. Their survival depended on those skills. It was considered childish and rude to ask a lot of questions.

The Canadian learning system is modeled on European systems, and European immigrants generally do very well in programs because the model is familiar. Asian people often do very well also, not because our systems are like theirs but because one aspect of their educational system is to do exactly what the teacher tells you to do, and to take responsibility for your own learning.

Some of the students who tend to do poorly in the system are the angry students, wherever they come from; we do not handle anger well as a culture. We push it away, in whatever ways we can. If race happens to be a factor creating that anger, then the system itself acts against those learners rather than trying to understand what the anger is about and working with the students in that space.

Intelligence tests and other forms of tests are other ways of separating out those who are different. At a conference some years ago, a Black psychologist proved his point by giving his audience a brief "Black" IQ test based on information most Black Nova Scotians would know. Many people failed miserably as they knew neither the terminology nor the cultural referents on which the test was based.

Another big problem in the schools has to do with teacher expectations. There is ample research to demonstrate that the expectations a teacher has for a learner affect how that learner does in school. According to James Battle in his book *Overcoming Racism and Achieving Success*, when a teacher decides that a learner is less than capable, for whatever reason, he or she will often change behaviour towards that learner in the following ways:

1. give him or her less direct instruction
2. have him or her sit farther away from the teacher's desk
3. ask him or her to do less work
4. provide him or her fewer opportunities to learn new material
5. call on him or her less frequently and when the teacher does, the questions are generally simple ones
6. provide him or her less time to respond to questions and give less help when answers are incorrect.

Another factor in systemic discrimination can be the choice of material chosen for instruction. Have you ever noticed how few women appear in history texts? It is as though women do not exist until the modern world. Yet if one is willing to dig deeply enough, one can find numerous examples of women in positions of leadership and talent in many areas of endeavour.

Similarly, how many Canadians know the achievements of Black Canadians? Everyone knows the expression "the real McCoy," but how many of us know that it comes from Elijah McCoy who invented a device which totally changed the way machinery could be lubricated. Many others tried to copy him without success and, to distinguish between the real item and the copies, the expression was born that his device was "the real McCoy." Elijah McCoy was a Black Canadian. Do people know of Lincoln Alexander who was the first Black Member of Parliament, the first Black cabinet minister, and the first Black lieutenant-governor? Do people know Rosemary Brown, the NDP member of the British Columbia legislature who so impressed those who knew her or listened to her speak? The first woman to start and edit a newspaper in Canada was also Black, Mary Ann Shadd in Ontario. And the list goes on. One very concrete action we can take in battling racism lies in acknowledging and teaching others about the achievements of people of colour in our own societies.

Institutional or systemic racism takes many forms which affect the ESL learner: word of mouth job recruitment that denies access to the newcomer; non-recognition of foreign credentials, regardless of the competency level to which they attest; and immigration policies which define family as nuclear and establish more immigration offices in some countries/continents than others, regardless of need or demand.

In our schools, we also have to teach learners to be critical in their reading of history and other material. When we read "massacre," we must realize that for the group who won that confrontation it was a victory, and we only call it a massacre because we accept the viewpoint of the authors of history that one group lost.

Our so-called justice system is another example of racism in action. In 1995 the Government of Ontario did a study of systemic racism in their justice system and discovered that Blacks were operating at a serious disadvantage. Findings included the following:

1. White people accused and charged for the same offense as Blacks were more likely to be released by officers and less likely to be detained after a bail hearing.
2. White people were more favourably treated by police officers although they were more likely than their Black counterparts to have a more serious criminal record.
3. Black people accused of crimes were more likely to be detained by police although they were less likely to have criminal records than their white counterparts.

The report was filled with more of the same.

This report has important ramifications for ESL educators because students are Somalians, Ethiopians, Cambodians, Vietnamese, Indians, and people of many races. If the learners are more likely to be stopped by a police officer because they look "different," they need to know that. If when they are stopped, they are harassed, they need to know how to deal with this situation in that moment or know how to lay a complaint, if that is what they decide to do. They need to know that, while they have to take responsibility for their own actions, things may happen to them that are not their fault and that they could have done little to prevent.

Similarly, racism affects many learners in the area of employment, both in getting a job and in advancing within a career. An acquaintance of mine once told me something that caught me quite by surprise as he is a gentle, pleasant person. He said, "Why should I hire someone of a different race when I can hire someone of the same race? Why make everyone in the office uncomfortable for no reason?" He could see nothing wrong with that statement, and I realized that his views, so openly expressed, were probably consistent with what many employers think and feel.

His response was an open invitation to affirmative action. Through affirmative action programs, people can get to know other people they have perceived as different from themselves thus providing an opportunity for their fears to melt away, leaving them with a broader comfort zone than they had before. My acquaintance's participation as host in a job training program for three months changed his views totally. (His placement was a highly intelligent young woman from Hong Kong who clearly did superior work and got along well with everyone in the office.)

Our students come to class with many stories of discrimination in the workplace. Learners who work in nursing homes have reported racial mistreatment from both staff and residents, for example. Many feel that they have to work twice as hard and be at least twice as nice to be recognized as being equal, a common experience for women in the recent past.

Responses to Allegations of Racism

Our society is very adept at rationalizing away any challenges to the ways we handle discomfort. I would hope that, by being aware at least of the typical ways in which we deflect allegations of racism, we might become more self-reflective and recognize when we ourselves or others are doing this. Dominelli offers the following typical patterns of response by those to whom racism is pointed out:

> *denial* – This response is based on the assumption that all racism is personal and that other forms of racism do not exist.
> *colour-blind strategies* – This common response is based on the belief that all people are the same and have similar problems, needs, and objectives.
> *patronization* – Many accept the principle of equality but put up a fierce resistance if the white power base is in any way threatened.
> *dumping strategies* – Some people lay the responsibility for resolving racism totally on the victims.
> *decontextualization strategies* – Many will acknowledge that racism exists but are sure that it has no place in their organization.

I have seen all of these strategies and probably have used most of them at one time or another and yet, until I saw them named, I did not recognize them for what they were.

Challenges to Teachers

Our perceptions are created by our experiences. Those of us who have little occasion to experience the ugly effects of racism tend to be less conscious of its existence and to think it is not a problem. Or, even if we are aware intellectually that racism exists, we may lack the emotive experience that a victim of racism possesses. So our need to develop our awareness is the first problem—to understand both the prevalence of racism and the many ways in which it is manifest in our society, particularly as it affects the learners with whom we work.

Secondly, we need to encourage people of all races to name their own experiences and to own their feelings about those experiences. I have met many people of colour who themselves deny that racism is a problem. I understand this in a way; by denying how racism affects them, they do not have to deal with it. It is easier to overlook incidents than to confront them. On the other hand, when you overlook a series of seemingly small assaults to your dignity, at what point do you lose your self-respect altogether? And what effect does denying one's own experiences have on others in terms of naming or denying their experiences? I am not suggesting that one should get riled up about every incident which has the potential of being racially motivated. What I am saying is that choice resides in consciousness and that denial has a way of shutting down our consciousness and therefore of limiting our choices.

Racism in the Classroom

Rather than ignore the effect racism has or can have on the learners with whom we work, we can choose to be as present to this reality as the learners will allow us to be, thereby freeing the learners to be themselves, to name and explore their issues, and to be prepared for possibilities which will confront them if they have not already done so.

I take a position which is seen by some as controversial. Be that as it may, my approach is practical. I believe there are two responsibilities we need to take as educators. One is to take a zero tolerance position on racism as it appears and to do everything in our power to promote the respect and dignity of all persons in our society. The other is to provide learners with as much knowledge and as many practical skills as we can in order that they can take personal accountability for their lives in any and all situations they encounter.

By accountability, I do not mean responsibility. The victim is not responsible for his/her victimization. However, accountability is a position one chooses which says, "What can I do to make this situation better for myself and those around me?" By choosing to use what power one has in a situation, one can mitigate the damage done by racism and choose not to let it destroy one's dignity and one's possibilities in life.

Here are some suggestions for what we might do in relation to our teaching:

- **Acknowledge** racism whenever we experience or observe it and take seriously the complaints we hear from those who feel they have been victimized.

- **Encourage** learners to talk about their experiences openly and explore possibilities with one another.
- **Accept** and **respect** each and every person in the classroom as they are.
- Have **faith** individually and collectively that we can heal and change our lives and our world.
- Be **willing** to admit our own shortcomings and work to change them.
- Be **open** ourselves about racial experiences and about our own prejudicial legacies.
- Give **permission** for each person to handle racial situations as best they can at the moment. (No one has all the answers. There is no one right or wrong in any given situation. The person who is in that situation has the right to make the best choice he or she can at that moment.)
- Endeavour to practise **balance** in your own responses to racism between the need for the individual to survive and be successful and the need to confront social injustice and create better alternatives for us all.
- **Prepare** learners for the real world and ensure that they know their choices and the possible consequences of those choices.
- As a professional, strive to **discover** racist structures, policies, and practises in our own profession and work to eliminate them.
- **Support** hiring policies which accept teachers with accents in order to have teachers of other races and cultures on the staff.
- **Ensure** that the content of your lessons acknowledges the contributions and successes of people of many races in your community.
- **Commit** to social change, advocacy, anti-racist education, and when necessary, confrontation of racist behaviors.
- **Understand** and be patient with those who need support and with those who need to change. Victims of racism often get snagged in bitterness and anger which further alienate them from the broader community. These reactions aggravate rather than heal the brokenness of society. At the same time, anger is a better response to racism than despair. To heal takes a long time, and we have to be patient and understanding with those who are in pain and who are justifiably angry.

Workshop Activity 1

Sit down with a group of people and recall times when you have become aware of your own stereotyping. Discuss the effects such stereotypes have on us and on the people we stereotype.

Workshop Activity 2

Reflect in writing on your earliest memories of awareness around race. How old were you? What happened? What conclusions did you draw from what happened?

Workshop Activity 3

Identify ten words or expressions, other than those I mentioned, in the English language which are themselves racist. If you are stuck, read for a time and these expressions will stand out in your reading.

For Further Reading

There are many, many books available on racism and some take very different perspectives than others. Here are some which I have found particularly insightful.

McKague, Ormond, Ed. 1991. *Racism in Canada*. Saskatoon: Fifth House Publishers.

> The broad selection of authors in this text represents many cultural perspectives and experiences and writings under the general headings of historical, structural, and personal racism. In one section, the authors look at the triple whammy when race, gender, and culture all combine to the alienation of some. Concluding articles, including one by Rosemary Brown, look at what can and is being done to resolve the problems.

Henry, Frances, Carol Tator, Winston Mattes, and Tim Rees. 1995. *The Colour of Democracy: Racism in Canadian Society*. Toronto: Harcourt Brace and Co., Canada.

> The chapters of this book nicely combine both theory and first-hand experience. The book is organized in four parts: perspectives on racism, racism in the public sector, racism in education and cultural institutions, and the impact of democratic racism on Canadian institutions. A must-read for anyone interested in this topic in Canada.

Cannon, Margaret. 1995. *The Invisible Empire: Racism in Canada*. Toronto: Random House of Canada.

> Written conversationally with many anecdotes, this book is a quintessentially Canadian snapshot of the politics of race in the country today. A writer with heart, this author spent years researching and writing about racism.

Berdichewsky, Bernardo. 1994. *Racism, Ethnicity, and Multiculturalism*. Vancouver: Future Publications.

> The author provides a succinct introduction to the reality of these themes in Canadian society and contrasts them with their counterparts in the United States.

Loney, Martin. 1998. *The Pursuit of Division: Race, Gender, and Preferential Hiring in Canada*. Montreal: McGill and Toronto: Kingston University Press.

> A controversial work, this book presents a very different view from that of the authors presented thus far. The author presents a well-researched position, contrary to the

analyses of radical feminism and Marxism, arguing that hiring should be decided on merit alone.

Pizanias, Caterina and James S. Frideres, Ed. 1995. *Freedom Within the Margins: The Politics of Exclusion*. Calgary: Detselig Enterprises Ltd.

In this edited collection of essays, the authors represent different disciplines and marginal groupings. The strength of the book is in the authenticity of its diverse voices exploring what it is to dwell on the margins.

Strong-Boag, Veronica, Sherrill Grace, Avigail Eisenberg, and Joan Anderson, Ed. 1998. *Painting the Maple: Essays on Race, Gender and the Construction of Canada*. Vancouver: UBC Press.

This unique book includes such diverse voices as the playwright Sharon Pollock and the novelist Denise Chong (who wrote *The Concubine's Children*). In addition to voices from literature, we hear a number of academic voices, and together we see a photo album of alternative visions of Canada. Many of the authors encourage the imagination of community. This book is one of my favourites in that hope infuses its pages.

CHAPTER 11

Social Class, Status, and the ESL Classroom

Questions to reflect upon:

- What have been your experiences of social class and status: as a youth, as an adult?
- How do these experiences compare with your perception of the social class and social status of the majority of your students in this country?
- To the best of your knowledge, how do the present social class and status of the learners you teach compare with their experience of social class and status in their own countries of origin?
- What behaviours and/or incidents in your classroom experience as a teacher do you attribute to social class?

Understanding the Sources of Diversity

While some ESL educators have acquired a well-developed understanding of the dimensions of social class in this country, many of us have not been exposed to such discourses. This chapter is written for those who still find social class a confusing and complex notion, and one to which they have not to date attended in their teaching practise.

Many of us have had a tendency to account for diversity in our classrooms by some combination of cultural difference and personality, but these are not the only factors that create diversity in our classrooms. Social class, gender, religion, age, amount and type of education, and many other personal characteristics all influence a person's behaviour, attitudes, values, and beliefs about life and about learning.

While we may have minimized the importance of recognizing and working with class differences in the classroom, this is not necessarily true of the learners, especially when they are learning with people from their own culture who have different class backgrounds. Just as we easily recognize those whose language and behaviour signals a different social background to our own, so do the learners recognize such differences readily in populations of their own culture. It is important for us to begin to gain some insight into the nature of social class as a phenomenon, and identify the ways in which it plays itself out in our classrooms. Then we can begin to ask ourselves how we can best work with this reality in ways that allow learners to become more critically reflective of their own views and choices—with one another, in their learning, and in their interactions within the broader society.

What Is Social Class?

Social class is the manner society has developed for valuing different groups of people with different backgrounds, values, and access to the resources within a society. I do not know of any society where it is not present in some form or other, although different societies certainly have different ways of defining and dealing with the concept. Nor do I particularly like this concept for it divides people from one another and has the unhappy result of some people having much more than others and some people suffering much more than others. However, social class is, I believe, a part of our reality that we need to better understand to find ways of minimizing and eventually eradicating its influence. It is a question of social justice.

Some theorists use economic measures to define class differences while others have a more complex way of defining those differences. Naiman in her book *How Societies Work: Class, Power, and Change in a Canadian Context* distinguishes between *class* and *status*. The author defines class as one's relationship to the means of production, a Marxist definition; and defines status as a more complex indicator including not only economic resources but also occupation, property ownership, income level, and public visibility, to name a few factors. Regardless of how we define class, it is important to recognize that some people feel superior or inferior to others due to the differences cited. In addition, regardless of their own awareness of differences, their access to resources and opportunities are also different.

To start with the familiar, let us look at our public schools. It is not uncommon for the schools in rich neighbourhoods to have international exchange programs for their students, or to organize international travel at some cost to the families of those students. A very few schools will do fundraising programs during the year for those families who do not have the resources to pay for their children to participate in such experiences. In that case, parents are expected to give time for those fundraising activities, time which may not be available to single parents, to parents working two jobs, or to those in poor health, for example. Inevitably, unless everyone in the school is in a high socioeconomic bracket, some children will feel excluded or embarrassed by their economic differences in this instance.

Many children seldom have any such extra-curricular experiences, unless they are fortunate enough to capture the heart of some benefactor who donates funds and/or organizes the community around such a project. The child who has been exposed to a solid reading culture, many experiences of travel, and the varied forms of recreation available to the wealthy is going to view the world and him- or herself very differently than a child whose world is confined to a two-room house with eight people living in it, one of whom may drink and beat another. These examples may represent two extremes, but the extremes are a helpful starting place in viewing the continuum of our collective experiences in the world.

In the ESL classroom, learners are very sensitive to body language and other non-verbal expressions of meaning. I recall a time when many Latin American refugees were in our classrooms. A group of students came to warn me that Maria Patricia (not her real name) was not who she professed to be. I asked what they meant by that. They told me not to believe her stories about being a teacher, being well off, and having servants in her country. Why not, I asked. They tried to explain that they could tell from her Spanish and from her actions that none of this could be true. I did not quite understand until one night we had a potluck dinner, and I saw Maria Patricia put her cigarette out on a soft linoleum floor in the kitchen. Another student gave me a look that said, "See, what we have been telling you. . . . ," and I realized that what they had said made sense. This woman was used to dirt floors. It was unlikely that she had the education or financial resources she claimed.

Some students, feeling the indignity of not knowing the language and not feeling they have control over their own destiny see a need to compensate by creating fantasies which they hope will lead others to believe that they are important people and therefore deserving of privilege. At the same time, some learners who did indeed have privileged status in their home countries have all the more pain here because they are not accorded that same status now. Not only are we in no position to know what their real backgrounds are, socially speaking, or to respond as they might hope, we also have a responsibility to introduce them to our society.

Social class is not entirely absent in North America, but it is unquestionably different from what the learners experienced in other countries. The classroom needs to be an egalitarian experience in which all learners, regardless of how much money they had or have, or how much they know or don't know, feel comfortable learning what they are able to learn and want to learn at this time. The bottom line is that everyone needs to feel respect and acceptance from others, and as long as each person is willing to afford those things to others, there is no reason not to expect them in return.

Social Class, Language, and Choice

We are teachers of language. Language and social class are also related. Our ability to use language is shaped by the ways in which the people around us use language. We can sometimes hear the differences in speaking between the child of university-educated professional parents, the child of a farm family, the child of a tradesperson, and the child of a family who is the third generation on social assistance. While there are many exceptions to these generalizations, depending on the personal preferences, values, and experiences of the individuals in these contexts, there is a tendency for people with more education and higher social status in society to have a higher level of standardized grammar and writing skill, a larger vocabulary, and a predisposition to valuing learning as an on-going part of the life experience.

A tradesperson may earn more money than a professional, but that money may get spent on alcohol, attendance at professional sports, a big motor boat for use at the lake in the summer, and a new four-wheel drive automobile every second year. The professional, on the other hand, may choose to spend her income on a Toyota, which is replaced every ten years, books, trips to various countries, and her children's participation in piano lessons and other cultural enrichments. While such choices do not in and of themselves create social class, they do tend to influence the individual's style and content of communication. What is worth talking about? What is worth doing? That, in turn, influences who the individual wants to communicate with. Groups are formed and those groups tend to develop a sense of their own superiority or inferiority in relation to other groups.

In addition, people who are educated and have strong networks of powerful people find life generally easier than those who lack knowledge and information. They have the expectation that their problems have a solution while people living in poverty often approach life with the expectation that they will have problems. In one low-income family, it is not uncommon to find financial, health, serious emotional, and even legal problems. Daily life is often experienced as a struggle from which there is no escape, and that is the life into which children are born and develop expectations for their own lives. While there are means in our society for a strong child to break out of that mold, most children do not and have a tendency to reproduce the same values and expectations which were present in their growing years.

How Does Social Class Influence the ESL Classroom?

There are two areas in which we need to ask this question. The first is in terms of the attitudes and behaviours each and every learner brings with him or her to the classroom, and the second is in terms of the society into which we are preparing these learners to function successfully.

The behaviours learners bring with them in relation to social class and gender have a strong influence on their interactions with other learners and with the teacher in the classroom. Mutual respect is an important facet of classroom interaction, and while we can attempt to mandate this by simply telling people what we expect, one cannot expect the average person to set aside years of feeling superior just because we say so. I have a great deal of compassion for learners I have taught who came from backgrounds in which they received a lot of personal respect or even homage because those learners may have a great deal of difficulty sitting beside and working together with those they perceive to be of lesser value than themselves. Some learners will even refuse to do pair work with anyone but the teacher because they perceive that they are wasting their time.

I remember a teacher, originally from China, who always treated me with great respect and even deference to my discomfort. Nonetheless, I respected her diligence and commitment to teaching, and I acknowledged her fluency in English. I was very surprised one day to observe the way in which she was talking, in Mandarin, to a student in another program we were offering. (The teacher did not know I was there or I am sure she would have behaved very differently.) She was sharp and condescending to the woman, who was also from China. The student behaved very deferentially and appeared fearful of this teacher, a behaviour I had never seen in the student before. Neither person appeared to be acting in character as I knew them, and I wanted to understand why.

I spoke with the student, whom I knew well, and I asked her why the teacher had been speaking to her so sharply. Did she know her? No, she had never met her before. The woman was very embarrassed by my question, and she answered by saying that, except for her father, the people in the program were the first people who had ever treated her with respect in her life. She was happy at the school because she felt like there was hope and said that her father wanted a different life for her. When the other teacher had questioned her in Mandarin, her accent and manner of speaking gave away her class background, and the teacher had simply responded to her as had all the other people she had known in her life. She said she was sorry I had seen this and told me not to worry about it. When I spoke to the teacher about what I had observed, she simply dismissed it as nothing and said I had misunderstood, but she too was clearly embarrassed that I had witnessed this. I later came to know this teacher better and learned that she was from a very old, respected family in China and that, in spite of Communism, she had retained the cultural knowledge and use of the language that had set her family apart for generations. She is normally very careful about her social register and goes out of her way to speak very respectfully to those who she perceives to have power, but, in this instance, she saw the woman as powerless.

Social register can and does play a role in the interactions between students and their willingness (or resistance) to working cooperatively in the classroom. It is actually an advantage to have several different races, cultures, and other diversities in the classroom because, for most learners, this is the reality they will face in their new country. I do not have any facile solutions to dealing with class problems when they arise. I do think, however, that we need to recognize such problems for what they are and not simply try to brush them aside and pretend that they are not there. For us to respect each and every learner in the class-room means we have to recognize their struggles and discomforts and acknowledge them, even when we expect them to rise above these problems. The student with a superiority complex may be more in need of our compassion than the student who has never had any illusions about who he is but is happy with himself and his life. The woman who expects that because she was a wealthy banker in her country, she can be a wealthy banker in Canada or the United States is in for a rude shock, and it may take years for her to realize that she needs to begin from a different frame of reference in her new surroundings. Some never accept this reality and die bitter, unfulfilled people.

When class differences create discord in class, different approaches are possible. Which one you use depends on what you feel comfortable with. Some teachers will talk with the individual creating the problem and try to explain to the learner some of the differences there are in living in a new country. Some try to prevent problems by discussing the issues in class before they arise and by being clear about the expecta-tions they have for the class participants. Some deal with problems between individuals with the whole class, and the learnings for one or two become learnings for all. This technique can be very effective, but it necessitates that you yourself be compassionate and non-judgmental towards the learners.

There is a big difference between disliking a behaviour and disliking the individual who is thus behaving. We have lost our ability to teach a learner when he knows we dislike him. Instead by being compassionate with an individual stuck in his own sense of superiority, we have a chance of enabling that learner to gently release that position and discover the joys of knowing people for who they are rather than for who we think they ought to be. I believe that every classroom is a place where we should be able to grow as individuals. That includes the language-learning classroom. We do not change because someone tells us we are bad. That just makes us defensive. We change when we see it as being in our interest to do so, when our former beliefs, attitudes, and behaviours no longer produce the results we want in our lives.

Workshop Activity I

The following scenarios are real. They are offered in order for the reader to reflect on how he or she might understand and respond to various situations. These scenarios are best used in discussion with a group of teachers.

1. A Russian woman who had been an opera singer in the former Soviet Union refuses to do any kind of pair or group work with her classmates, none of whom are from Eastern Europe. She has stated there is no value in this activity.

2. A woman from Mexico is learning little in the class. She is from a wealthy family in the Chiapas area, where many people like her have been endangered by revolutionaries. Her family insisted that she come here with her husband and children to live until the rebellion is put down. In class, she cannot seem to concentrate and is very intolerant of the other students.

3. An older Vietnamese man participates little in the class, sitting quietly and staring off into space. The fingernails of his baby fingers are very long and pointed. He does not socialize with the other students, even those who are Vietnamese.

4. A thirty-six-year-old woman in your employability class has a dream of one day becoming a bank manager. Her English skills are minimal and she has only three years of schooling in China. She learns very slowly and lacks effective study skills. She is very determined and has really changed her appearance since she started the class. She has begun to wear makeup, which she applies very tastefully, and to dress in attractive feminine but business-like clothes each day.

5. An older Sikh man in your class is being taken care of by two younger Sikhs, a man and a woman who are also in the class. These learners do his homework assignments and intervene with the answers when he is asked a question. He takes all this as his due and brushes aside any suggestion on your part that he needs to participate if he wants to learn. The others tell you that he is the priest at the temple as if that should explain everything. This class is a university methodology course in Heritage Languages and is given for credit.

6. A Filipina woman in an evening class expresses her anger at co-workers who won't do what she tells them to do. You ask if she is their supervisor. She says no, looks uncomfortable, and then blurts out, "But I am older and I am educated. They should do what I say."

For Further Reading

Ng, Roxana. 1988. *The Politics of Community Services: Immigrant Women, Class and State*. Toronto: Garamond Press.

> This text is a superb glimpse inside an agency serving immigrant women and shows the ways in which our social construction of "class" serves to keep the immigrant woman outside of the mainstream, in spite of the best of intentions to the contrary.

Naiman, Joanne. 1997. *How Societies Work: Class, Power and Change in a Canadian Context*. Concord, ON: Irwin Publishing.

> A readable and well-written introductory sociology text, which differs from others of its kind partly because it is grounded in Canadian reality and partly because the author writes in an interesting and lucid manner that makes her topics accessible to beginning learners.

Creese, Gillian. 1999. *Contracting Masculinity: Gender, Class, and Race in a White-Collar Union 1944-1994*. Don Mills, ON: Oxford University Press.

> This text provides an in-depth study over a fifty-year period of how privilege or lack of privilege are differentially produced, reproduced, and challenged in an office environment. The author gives substance to theory in this well-researched work.

CHAPTER 12

Gender and Sexual Preference in the ESL Classroom

Questions to reflect upon:

- If you have a class of two men and twelve women, who do you think gets more "air time" in class, generally speaking?
- Can you think of subjects women are not comfortable discussing in a class with men?
- In a class of all men, what would likely be different, especially if the teacher were a man?
- Can you think of types of classes where you feel it would be inappropriate for the teacher to tell the students he was gay (or she was lesbian)? Why or why not?
- What kind of language is usually taught in ESL classrooms and for what contexts? Conversely, what are the contexts we tend not to teach? Why?

Gender and sexual preference are placed together in one chapter for convenience, not because they are any more related to each other than social class or racism; all of these personal characteristics have to do with power and privilege in our society. Gender refers to the state of one's male- or femaleness and how that state influences one's experience of being alive. While we may be born genetically male or female, the experience of that quirk of fate is socially constituted. We are concerned with the implications that has for the ESL classroom.

Sexual orientation has to do with one's sexual preference for and attraction to the same gender or its opposite. As with gender, one's experience of sexual orientation has to do with the manner in which people understand and accept (or do not accept) one's preference.

I do not profess to being an expert on either of these topics. I hesitate to include them because they are controversial and because there is a lot of good reference material available. I have to include them, however, because as ESL educators we are called upon to be discerning in our response to the realities—past, present, and future—of those we teach. Whatever decisions we make in regard to these and other topics must, I believe, be made in the best interests of those we teach. This calls upon us to set aside our own judgments and limitations and try to see what is indeed most appropriate at any given time for a particular group of learners. To that end, I seek to expand my own knowledge of topics such as these and to encourage you to do likewise.

Women's Classes

In the nineties, we saw a substantial recognition of the role and importance of having women's classes in ESL, a model few of us saw prior to that time. In Canada, the federally funded language program LINC (Language Instruction for Newcomers),[1] which was created in 1992, recognized the need for such classes. The government, with the support of most educators across the country, saw women as a group in need of special support. They recognized that women were most often the ones responsible for childcare and that they often lacked funds to pay others to provide care for their children while they attended school. For that reason, childcare was built into the funding for women's classes in LINC. Secondly, because in the past immigrant women were most often the ones left at home to take care of the family, this resulted in the presence of large numbers of citizens who had somehow attained citizenship without ever learning the language.

The government wanted to break this pattern and felt that by changing the policy so that men and women could both attend classes early upon their arrival, their integration would be more timely and more effective. (Unfortunately, this change in policy did nothing for the backlog of women who were still at home or in workplaces where they speak their own language. The federal government maintains that these women are the responsibility of the provinces, while some provinces say that if they did not receive language training when they arrived, it remains the responsibility of the federal government. In other words, women have not been a funding priority at any level of government in some provinces.)

There is another argument in defense of the policy of having women's classes. Any of us who have taught ESL for some time have had couples in our classes. In most cases, one person in the couple has taken the initiative on behalf of the other, sometimes because that person had more fluency and sometimes because it was understood to be his or her role. Men often assume the role of leader, putting the women in a position where they are hesitant to ask questions, to appear ignorant, or to offer their active participation. (This is not to say that some women will not take the more dominant role. I am more concerned, however, with those women who see it as culturally inappropriate to do so when their husband is present.) I think, for example, of the Afghan women, some of whom had husbands who did not want them coming to class at all for fear they would become independent like North American women. Those same husbands were willing to let their wives come to women's classes because, at least there, other men would not set eyes upon their wives.

There is also content that needs to be covered in a safe, all-female environment. Some might argue that such content can be taught in special sessions without organizing special classes. (Many of us did that when there was no other option, but that meant that we were choosing when the topics were to be covered, and our timing was not always that of the learners.) Such topics as breast examinations and Pap smears to prevent cancer are examples of topics most women would feel uncomfortable talking about in a class with men. However, in my experience, these are not the only important topics to cover with a women's class.

Abuse is a huge concern for many, and immigrant women need to know what rights they have in this country and what services are available should they need and choose to exercise those rights. I have had some strong reactions from individuals and even cultural groups in making this information known to classes. One Latin American group accused our school of trying to break up families. This was far from our intent. However, our first priority was ensuring the safety of women and children while honouring a woman's right to choose. One ethnic group, however, did not see it that way. Some individual men were also very angry that we told women about women's shelters and how to access them.

Spousal abuse is not a straightforward issue by any means. Cultures have operated as they have for hundreds of years and more. When refugees are suddenly uprooted from everything they have known and plunged into, what is for them, utter chaos, we cannot expect them to embrace our values overnight, if at all. Immigrants who have chosen to come to Canada may also be unaware of the extent to which the cultural values of this society vary from the ones they left behind. At the same time, part of our job is to introduce people both to the laws of the land and to the cultural norms that accompany those laws. Then, it is up to the individuals what they do with that information.

When it comes to the safety of children, however, most teachers take a different position, namely that the safety of the child comes first. If this is the case, I believe that we have a responsibility to tell our learners up front that if we become aware that a child is being neglected or abused, we will report it. In addition, we need to be sure, even if we must use translators or interpreters, that they understand what we mean (legally) by neglect and abuse.

Women's classes are most effective when we take the time and energy to build a high degree of trust and community in the classroom so that people feel safe telling their concerns and asking their questions, whatever those might be. The learners have to know that we are not there to impose our values on them, unless we state so as mentioned above. I feel comfortable knowing that I give people both the information and the support to make their own choices. We have to be genuine in giving our support, whether or not we agree with the women's decisions. It can be heart-rending to take a woman to a shelter when she is badly beaten, only to have her return home a week later to more of the same, but it is not our place to judge anyone. That woman is doing the best she can in some difficult circumstances, which we probably understand very little. It is important to treat her with the same respect *after* the decision to return home as we did when she had decided to leave. She may leave six times, and only on the seventh time, decide to try it alone—a decision she may not have been able to make if we had given her the cold shoulder each time she went back.

In the school that I directed for ten years, we believed strongly in community-building within the school. We knew that if the women came to know and care for and about one another, they would have support when their classes were finished. We knew also that if they could create community in the school's multicultural setting with one another, they had come a long way in being at home in this multicultural country. In addition, of course, learners learn more and faster when they are relaxed and happy in the classroom.

I have often thought it would be useful for men to have men-only classes too, taught by men who can introduce their students to our cultural ways and deal with their concerns in an open fashion, but that idea has never met with much agreement from funders. Nonetheless, you might have better luck!

Homosexuality in the Classroom

The topic of homosexuality needs to be approached from two perspectives: the homosexual learner and the homosexual teacher. The preference for romantic and sexual relations with people of the same sex is a culturally loaded topic. This is not to say that homosexuality is not present in most cultures, but how it is handled and regarded by members of a culture varies from acceptable to abhorrent. I believe that our handling of this sensitive subject needs to be based upon two primary factors: the ability of the learners to handle it openly or not, and the ability of the teacher to do so.

In our culture, it is a question of values. There are many teachers for whom homosexuality is no more than a way of being, a fact of the universe, and they would have no problem dealing with this subject as easily as with any other. There are others, however, who view homosexuality as a sin, and it would be difficult, if not impossible, for those individuals to address this topic and its related concerns in any kind of fair and objective manner. It is better to leave the subject alone than to convey disrespect and intolerance (or worse) in discussing it.

When we are working with learners who are educated and aware of this reality, it is important to talk about homosexuality openly so they become aware of attitudes in our society. They need to understand that North American society is in a transition and that, while many people are quite accepting of a homosexual person, there are others who are not, and that it can be dangerous in some situations for homosexuals to convey that preference openly. They also need to understand that the law, in most cases, protects homosexual people.

However, if we are teaching individuals who have never heard of homosexuality, and might find the idea horrific (and there are people for whom this is true), we risk alienating them completely and adversely affecting their ability to learn the language with us. With these learners, timing is significant.

I know of a lesbian teacher who decided that she wanted to tell her students of her sexual preference because she wanted to be friends with them and felt that the truth was necessary for that to happen, an understandable thought on her part. The teacher wanted them to meet her partner and her daughter and to know that they were a family, just like they themselves were part of families. She was tired of pretending. One of her colleagues, an immigrant woman, was horrified by this idea, remembering that when she herself had come to Canada, she had had no idea what a homosexual was and had been scandalized by the mere idea.

Their supervisor consulted colleagues in the settlement community who consistently said that their cultural communities would never register at that school if word got out that one of the teachers was a homosexual. That viewpoint was expressed strongly by representatives of three different ethnic groups, all of whom had lived in Canada for some time. With much persuasion, the teacher agreed to keep her secret to herself, and I have no doubt that she did so with great sorrow. That is a very hard choice to make.

This same teacher also confided to me that she had revealed her sexual orientation to a former student whom she believed to be a lesbian in need of coming out. This disclosure concerned my colleague and me because we had previously observed a sudden change in this student's behaviour; she had begun acting sexually aggressive towards me and my colleague, in spite of our clear rebuffs. Only after the teacher's revelation did we have an idea what had prompted this change. Because we did not know how to understand this learner's distressing behaviour, we had treated it as a bad joke. Only much later did we learn that this teacher was encouraging the learner to be open about her sexuality.

This is a dilemma. On the one hand, I can understand the teacher's wanting to be supportive of her former student, if she was, in fact, a lesbian who had been fearful of owning that aspect of herself. But was this teacher going to be there over the long term, supporting this woman if her whole community, even her own family rejected her? If a teacher is going to intervene in a personal situation of this magnitude, she had better be very sure that she has the wisdom and the commitment to follow through on what she starts. Personally, I would not want that responsibility.

Homosexuality is a sensitive topic but one with which we as professionals must, at some point, come to terms. Our guidelines should be based on what is in the best interests of the learners. If the notion of homosexuality is repugnant or even unknown to them, why not let it wait for later in their adjustment to come to terms with that idea? It has nothing to do with right and wrong; it has to do with how we see our responsibility to the learners. I see it as my responsibility to ease their transition to this country and this culture, and at times, that means I must make some difficult judgment calls.

AIDS and Its Prevention

Both TESOL and TESL Canada have encouraged their memberships to teach learners about safer sex and the prevention of AIDS. It seems obvious to me that if we are going to do this, homosexuality is definitely going to come up in the conversation. However, we can discuss the fact of homosexuality in our society without saying that one or more of the teachers is a homosexual, a disclosure which may certainly compromise that individual's ability to teach some students effectively. While homosexual activity is not the only means of contracting AIDS, it is the most common method of transmission, especially now that there is so much better care in the handling of blood and blood products. Again, we have to use our judgment. When is the best time to teach this material? Only you can determine the answer to this question, based on what you know of the students and their priorities.

Workshop Activity I

There is a wealth of material available in the community on the topics of partner abuse and AIDS. Choose one of these topics and gather some materials together for use in the classrooms in which you teach. Women's shelters are a good source of information on abuse. Many shelters welcome professional visitors, but you have to telephone first as the addresses are not listed for obvious reasons. (In addition, you will be asked to sign a commitment not to disclose the whereabouts of the shelter to anyone.) Public health units, libraries, and various AIDS agencies will have information on AIDS. Discuss with colleagues your comfort or discomfort with these topics.

Workshop Activity 2

Call your local shelter and ask them to mail you any written information they have on the signals of abuse. We need to learn what abuse is, as it is not only physical, and we need to know how to recognize potential victims of abuse.

For Further Reading

Strong-Boag, Veronica, et al, Ed. 1998. *Painting the Maple: Essays on Race, Gender and the Construction of Canada*. Vancouver: UBC Press.

> This most interesting collection of essays covers a wide range of disciplines. We read alternative visions of Canada from a playwright, a lesbian author, a novelist, a historian, and many others. In addition to helping us understand our own complex society, this book invites us to imagine and re-imagine community. A carefully crafted integration of diverse voices.

Creese, Gillian. 1999. *Contracting Masculinity: Gender, Class, and Race in a White-Collar Union, 1944–1994*. Don Mills, ON: Oxford University Press.

> While the majority of people in society probably think of gender as a simple biological distinction, the reader of this text goes away understanding gender as a social construct in the same way as race or social class. In spite of major advancements in the liberation of women in our societies, many people still have the image of a "woman" when they hear: secretary, sewing machine operator, or housekeeper, and of a "man" when they hear: doctor, lawyer, or banker. Creese effectively shows how "social life is actively constituted through negotiation, resistance, and accommodation, with experiences mediated through historically situated forms of understanding."

Endnotes

1. At the end of 1997 LINC began to disappear as the provinces took over primary responsibility for language instruction for newcomers to the country.

Being and Becoming Professional

CHAPTER 13

Professional Issues

Questions to reflect upon:

- What does it mean to be a professional?
- Who influences the policies which govern your teaching, and how can you influence them?
- How do policy-makers make informed decisions?
- How do you see the role of a good professional association?
- What are the inherent pitfalls in advocating for the learners?
- Why do ESL teachers typically have so little job security?

Being a Professional

To say that one is a professional generally indicates that the following statements are true:
- She or he is paid to work in a profession.
- She or he is educated and/or trained so as to have good skills to do that work.
- She or he qualifies for active membership in the appropriate professional association.
- She or he behaves in a manner generally perceived to be appropriate for a member of that profession.

Professionals are usually respected in the wider community, unless they behave in some way that undermines that respect. Furthermore, through their professional associations, they are normally accorded a role in contributing to the development of policies with regard to how that profession carries out its duties for the common good.

In that TESL is relatively new as a profession, until recently it has not had in place the kinds of documentation (e.g., codes of ethics, manner of disciplining violations of professional codes of conduct, manner of appealing disciplinary action, etc.) of other professional organizations. In many areas such documentation is still not in place.

In this chapter, we seek to understand what it means to be a professional and what steps we need to take in the near future to professionalize our work. To do so will go a long way towards giving ESL teachers the credibility to fight conditions of job insecurity, low wages, and few or no benefits—realities which have plagued this field since its inception.

TESL Training and Education

The job of ESL teacher has changed greatly in the past twenty-some years and it is continuing to change as we now talk about accreditation and program standards. When I began teaching ESL, there were few TESL programs and those of us hired to teach ESL in those days were most often certified as French as a Second Language teachers, unless we came from a city that had a TESL program. That has changed a great deal.

Now all of the provinces have some sort of TESL training, and the majority of TESL jobs require teachers to have some sort of training and/or experience. Institutional programs typically look for a valid teacher's certificate in the province where a person is applying as well as some TESL training. In Alberta, for example, this training may be a graduate diploma in TESL or a bachelor's degree with a major or minor in TESL. In addition, government-sponsored programs usually favour those who are accredited by their provincial association, and the systems of accreditation vary widely throughout the country. In other words, if one wants to work as a professional in this field, training and education as well as accreditation are now widely available and taken for granted in many teaching contexts.

Accreditation and Certification

Accreditation is not the same as certification. *Accreditation* is the recognition by a professional association of one's credentials. In granting accreditation, an association is telling the community that an association of a person's peers deems that individual worthy of employment in the field. *Certification*, on the other hand, is the recognition by an outside body, usually a government, of that person's credentials. Therefore a typical ESL teacher in Alberta, for example, working in an institution might have a Bachelor of Education degree from a university, a graduate diploma in TESL, a teacher's certificate from the province as well as accreditation from his or her professional association.

Accreditation in ESL, while becoming increasingly available, is nonetheless a challenging and controversial issue, primarily because the contexts in which ESL teachers work are so varied and bring such different demands. In addition, when one looks at the so-called typical qualifications a teacher brings to the job, one has to wonder why there is so little job security, such low wages, and poor (if any) benefits in many of these contexts. These factors contribute to the controversy surrounding accreditation and the ways associations are dealing with that controversy.

Accreditation sets out the conditions or terms of reference for the accredited professionals. These conditions normally include both training requirements and teaching experience in acceptable contexts (e.g., certified schools or programs), providing clear minimum standards for each. The teacher submits an application together with proof of employment and qualifications, and a committee of peers reviews this documentation and decides whether the individual meets the criteria or not. The accrediting body sometimes requests further documentation before ruling. Most accreditation systems have what are called "grandfathering" clauses to recognize those teachers who have long experience but may not meet the minimum criteria for training.

One of the dangers I have seen in approving accreditation standards offered to professional association memberships is that, too often, individuals look first to their own individual right to belong and, once they see that they are "safe", often fail to consider the implications for the profession in the future. Many such individuals get in on "grandfathering" clauses and rest content. They may not appreciate the numbers of excellently prepared individuals who may not qualify later on, although these teachers might have a great deal more to offer a particular context than someone who has all the needed credentials but no experience or interest in the work context. What about experienced teachers from other provinces? What about teachers coming from other countries? What about the need to have men and women of other races, cultures, and languages on our teaching staffs?

Because accreditation is still a relatively new phenomenon in most provinces and states, there is still some uncertainty as to how it will be regarded by employers and funders. Funders like the idea of accreditation because it turns over to someone else responsibility for the quality of teaching, and some employers like it for the same reason. Other employers, however, will continue to follow their own guidelines in hiring the best possible people for specific jobs, as long as their funding is not tied to their use of accredited personnel. The inherent difficulties of insisting on accredited teachers are not unique to ESL; one sees them in education generally. However, teaching immigrant seniors in a settlement agency is very different from teaching immigrant professionals in an institution or immigrant food-processing workers in a plant. The skills required in these three situations are very different, and accreditation tends to acknowledge only those skills required in the institutional setting. As professionals, it is up to each one of us to examine what our own professional associations have defined for accreditation purposes and to put pressure to bear to ensure that those standards are broad or varied enough to encompass everyone who will be affected by them.

Membership and Participation in a Professional Association

Most of us will join one or more professional associations to include that information in our resumés to have access to the annual conference, and/or to receive the accompanying professional journal. While membership has many advantages, the greatest benefit by far is that accrued by active participation.

Participation is empowering. When you catch yourself saying, "Why don't *they* do such and such," remind yourself that it is not *they* but *we*. You can participate in so many ways. Serving on the board of the local or provincial association is a wonderful way to gain understanding of policy issues and to have a say in the development of those policies. You will learn skills that will benefit you in many ways in the future. You can get to know colleagues, not only in your own area but throughout the country, and those relationships can bring untold benefits to your career and your life. If that does not appeal to you, you might want to volunteer to help organize a conference. That brings similar benefits with a shorter commitment. Or, you might want to volunteer to present a workshop or presentation to such a conference.

I hear so many teachers saying that they have nothing to offer others, that everyone knows what they know, but that is simply not true. We are all different and we all have some things we do well and others we could improve. If you are nervous about doing something alone, get together with a friend and do something together. No one expects you to be perfect, only to share what you know and believe to be true.

Getting and Staying Informed

Part of being a professional is staying on top of what is going on. We make victims out of ourselves when we do not care enough to know what is going on, to say what we think, or to stand up for what we believe to be right. It is sad to hear teachers expressing their disgust or frustration about policy decisions that reared their heads as possibilities long before they became realities when I know that such individuals expressed no concern about these developments in the early stages. We have a tendency to trust our policy-makers until they do something to destroy that trust, and then we complain but take no accountability for what has happened. Time and again this sets us up for similar frustrations.

We can be informed by reading our professional newsletters, by attending meetings to hear about what is going on, by asking questions, by visiting the national websites, and by entering into discussions with our colleagues and administrators either in person or on-line. When we go to the annual conference, do we go to the annual general meeting? No matter what time of day these AGMs are held, it is difficult to get sufficient numbers of members to come to the meetings. Our participation in these meetings ensures that we have had the opportunity to speak and be heard about important policy initiatives.

Our administrators attend a lot of meetings on a more regular basis, and they generally know what is going on in decision-making at government levels, but they may not share this information unless they know we are interested. Show your interest; volunteer to be part of committees and focus groups when given the opportunity. In this way you will not be caught by surprise when a new policy is announced.

E-mail has opened up a whole new world of communication. E-mail is a fast, inexpensive way to stay in contact with people no matter where they live. It is useful to maintain contacts in other provinces, states, and even countries, and you can use the information colleagues share with you to make your impact on policy development both locally and regionally.

Ethical Conduct and Copyright Legislation

In Chapter 4, ethics were discussed in some detail. One aspect not discussed was adherence to copyright legislation. It has become a serious problem in our field that so many teachers disregard copyright laws, and photocopy handouts for their students rather than purchasing class sets of materials for classroom use. Teachers rationalize this practise by citing the low budgets they have for materials and their desire to give learners the resources they need to support their learning. However, these teachers probably do not understand the low profit margin with which most publishers produce ESL materials, especially in Canada where the market is small.

Illegal photocopying may well smother the future publication of Canadian ESL materials. Two large publishers have already announced that they will not be publishing any new Canadian ESL materials because they are losing money, and they believe this is due to massive photocopying of existing materials. Those of us who remember the frustration of having to use American and British materials when there were no Canadian ESL materials are probably more respectful of the laws as well as the efforts publishers have recently made to produce materials relevant to our Canadian context. Younger teachers do not have this context and often fail to see the logical consequences of their actions. Both teachers and administrators need to find ways of enforcing the copyright legislation so that we may regain what we are losing in the way of Canadian materials.

Understanding and Influencing Policy

I have always found it interesting that learners who were semi-literate, but were also refugees from countries where they had participated in a revolution could have more awareness of politics than their teachers, with all their education and advantage. In Western society, most of us have been conditioned to trust our governments and elected representatives while at the same time we have been taught that "healthy criticism" is part of the democratic process. Government policy is cast with the same suspicious light, therefore, as *politics*, a word with the same root. If one looks back to the Latin and Greek roots, one finds that the words come to us from roots which mean "citizenship," from the Greek root *polis* which meaning "city." At what point, I wonder, did we lose sight of the participatory aspects of policy-making? At what point did we surrender decision-making to those we call civil servants and about whom we love to complain?

In my experience, the majority of civil servants are well-intended individuals eager to make good decisions about policy. However. they have two major obstacles with which to contend. The first is the political climate in which they work. No matter what they might believe personally, they take their instruction from the elected representatives who determine larger policies, budget guidelines, and general directions for their departments. The second is information, or rather a dearth thereof. They are not working directly in the field; we are. If we do not find ways to inform our civil servants as to what the reality is in our classrooms and in the lives of the learners, it is quite unfair to expect them to know.

We can become partners with these individuals in several ways. One is through our professional associations. Both politicians and civil servants are eager to co-operate with and listen to what our associations have to say. They need the information, and politically they need the support of these organizations and their members for they need to be seen as collaborative. If you have occasion to meet these individuals or work with them on a committee or a project, you have the opportunity to form friendly collegial relationships with them. These relationships can provide an open channel to give them information when it is appropriate, and to seek information from them when you need it. That dialogue is healthy for all concerned.

In case not everyone is aware of how policies evolve, let me share a few things I have learned. When a letter is sent to the Minister of a department, or when an invitation is made to a minister to speak, it is virtually never the Minister per se who answers that letter or prepares the speech. It is a civil servant designated to prepare these communications because he or she has the most relevant information. In all probability, the letter is first opened by the Minister's executive assistant and is then forwarded to a departmental staff member, who reads it and drafts a response. The assistant makes it his or her place to become informed as to the contents of the letter, so that when he presents it to the Minister for signature, he can answer any questions which may be asked at that time. In the case of an invitation to speak, the Minister is briefed by the assistant, who has made a point of gathering all relevant information and is either drafting a speech or having a speechwriter do so. When members of the professional association have made a point of being in regular communication with the appropriate staff in the related departments, chances are much greater that government policy will be based on accurate information.

So, if we want to influence policy at that level, we need first to be well-informed ourselves and to collaborate with others in our association. We have much more power to be heard as a group than we do as individuals. Secondly, we have to be diplomatic but at the same time clear and assertive. While we all know that angry confrontation alienates people and should be used as a last resort rather than a common strategy, I have seen many examples of fearful executives unwilling to say anything which might be construed as disagreeing with a policy, lest such disagreement alienate the politicians. This behaviour is read as weakness by politicians who then cease to listen to what we have to say.

We can be polite and strong at the same time; the key is to know what we are talking about. To take a stand based on inadequate information, or worse yet, false information, is a sure route to killing our credibility as individuals and as organizations. We have to do our homework very thoroughly before we take a position and make it public. When we do this and approach our politicians respectfully and co-operatively, they are likely to welcome our information and suggestions, especially if we have taken care to point out subtly how our recommendations are in the interests of those to whom we are speaking.

Best Practices and Program Standards

Best Practices and *Program Standards* are terms that have, in the past few years, become increasingly familiar across North America. Familiarity, however, does not mean consistency. People use these terms quite differently and often in overlapping ways. For purposes of this discussion, I am defining them as follows:

Best Practice Guidelines are statements a group of people use to describe excellence within their organization. They are used within the organization to evaluate and make improvements. *Program Standards* are similar statements, but they are used by *external* bodies to define expectations of organizations receiving funding. They are used to talk about accountability and to grant or withhold funds.

Best Practice Guidelines are often used as a preliminary step towards Program Standards in order to get organizations thinking about how they define excellence for their own purposes. Program Standards tend to be more definitive and are presented as minimum standards whereas Best Practice Guidelines may be written as ideals. Because Program Standards have to be assessed by someone, there is pressure to define them in ways which are easily measurable.

Categories within both Best Practice and Program Standards include the following: staffing, intents/goals/objectives, resources, facilities, activities, evaluation, curriculum, professional development, and many others. Best Practice Guidelines and Program Standards can be very valuable, providing that there is a good process for their development. Presenting these recommendations from the top down is seldom effective as they are often seen as threatening. Taking the time, however, to allow a group of people to develop these standards and guidelines together is respectful of the ability of professionals to define excellence in their own terms and provides the opportunity for individuals to develop awareness of what excellence is and how it may be achieved and evaluated. Creating guidelines and/or standards can be initiated either by professional associations or by government funders. What matters is the participation and sense of ownership by all who will be affected by such documents.

Here are some samples of how the two types of documents might compare:

Best Practice Guidelines	Corresponding Program Standards
Staffing:	**Staffing:**
All staff are respectful of all people regardless of race, religion, gender, age, or other difference.	(Many programs would not deal with these equity issues because it is hard to measure or demonstrate their presence or absence.)
All staff are qualified for the area of teaching to which they are assigned.	All institutional teaching staff have a valid teaching certificate, accreditation from the provincial association, and a minimum of five university TESL courses.

Best Practice Guidelines	Corresponding Program Standards
Curriculum: Each program has a curriculum document which lays out the intents of the program and the ways in which those intents may be realized through resources and activities appropriate to the needs of the learners. There are ample opportunities in the program for learners to participate in defining their own learning needs and preferred means of achieving their goals.	**Curriculum:** Each program has a curriculum document which lays out the intents of the program and the ways in which those intents may be realized through resources and activities appropriate to the needs of the learners. Staff policy documents have a clear policy of promoting learner participation in making the curriculum relevant to the needs of individual learners. This document is given to all learners as well as all teaching staff in the program.
Program evaluation: Students evaluate the program at the end of each course. Teachers are evaluated annually and given feedback on their teaching practice.	**Program Evaluation:** At the end of each session, learners are invited to evaluate their program and their instructors. Such information is collected anonymously and shared in written form with teaching staff. In addition, all instructors are evaluated annually and given feedback in writing.

In the samples given, we can see that the criteria for being included in the right hand column is measurability whereas we can afford to be a little more idealistic in the left hand column.

I have been very fortunate to have been actively involved in the making of both sets of guidelines within my province. I say fortunate because I now have a keen sense of ownership of both documents, and I also understand much better how others see what is important and what is not. We were also very fortunate in Alberta to have a provincial funder with a keen appreciation for process and skill in using it.

Until we actually talk about the quality of our practise as a group of educators, we may have a tendency to assume that everyone values the same things we do, and that is not necessarily so. By engaging in dialogue around what is important enough to be seen as minimal, we come to situate our own practise in relation to that of others. In Alberta, the Best Practices and later the Program Standards were both done through the provincial association, ATESL, with funding from the province. In both cases there was a strong consultative process. The final decisions for the Program Standards were made by a committee representative of all the sectors offering ESL programs: provincial institutions, school boards, settlement agencies, other non-governmental agencies, and private schools. The views of practising teachers were listened to, and an attempt was made to come up with a document that almost everyone could live with. I believe that the very process of forming these documents raised the level of excellence at which practitioners now see themselves working in this province.

Wages, Benefits, and Job Security

ESL teachers of adults continue to be one of the least secure, lowest-paid of the teaching professions, and many still have no benefits. Why is it that teachers who are so highly qualified continue to be in this situation?

There are several factors at work here. Governments are unwilling to create job security for teachers whose futures are so unknown due to the fact that immigration policy and world events are constantly changing. While that may explain the need to keep some teachers on short-term contracts, that does not explain why there are large numbers of teachers who have had virtually continuous employment for many years on short-term contracts. Nor does it explain in any manner why ESL teachers receive such low wages relative to teachers with similar credentials working in other subject areas. Nor does it account for the failure of governments to fund benefits except in the case of unionized teachers.

I had always assumed that our poor working conditions were somehow tied to the fact that we were working with adult learners and believed that ESL teachers working in public schools did not suffer these injustices. Then, one day, I heard such a teacher complaining about how lonely she felt teaching ESL in a public school. She believed that her status was at the bottom of the barrel, that other teachers did not see that it required expertise to teach English to immigrant learners. This lack of respect and valuing seems to be further borne out in the many instances in which ESL teachers have bumped by math or science teachers when cutbacks have to be made.

Is it possible that people who teach immigrant learners are accorded a status similar to that accorded by many to those immigrants themselves?

We often work with learners who enter into the labour market at the bottom rungs. Immigrants expected to drive taxis, clean toilets, sew our jeans, and slaughter our meat—the jobs no one else wants. All too often, the men and women doing these jobs have qualifications that greatly exceed those of the jobs they are doing but for reasons of accent, foreign credentials, and racism, they are unable to find suitable work in their new countries. I don't want to believe this but there is a lot of evidence to suggest that it is true. It is more than possible that our ongoing struggle for equal pay, benefits, and job security has much to do with the larger social structure.

The other factor I have seen is gender. By far, the greatest number of ESL teachers are women, and many of these women are married without the same need for income that a single woman or male head of a household needs to survive. I have had experiences where attempts to unionize teaching staff have been thwarted by the apathy of those teachers who have little or no need to earn a living through their work. Men and single women, however, either live with the low income and uncertainty because they are committed to the field, or they move on to other careers where there is better pay and more stability.

Advocacy

Many of us, as individuals and as members of associations, have been involved in various ways in advocating on behalf of those we teach. These actions might be as simple as calling a landlord and demanding to know why someone is asked to pay a monthly fee for use of the mailbox in the front of the building, or calling to request that utilities not be cut off when someone has not paid their bill and needs to make arrangements to pay. Or they might take the form of participating in consultations with the federal government for more liberal immigration policies which take into account the manner in which many cultures define family—as extended rather than nuclear.

We need to consider two issues before deciding whether or not to advocate for the learners we teach. The first question to ask ourselves is in whose interest it is. We have all heard the old adage about it being wiser to teach a man to fish than to catch the fish and give it to him. Yet it is one thing to agree with that and quite another to take an hour to teach someone to do something you could do yourself in five minutes or less.

Expedience might be a factor in considering what we need to do, but the settlement agencies have a mandate to do exactly the kind of tasks we so often do ourselves. Is that knowledge present when we make a decision as to what action to take? In some cases, it is simply easier and faster to do it ourselves, but is it better? I think we all need to caution ourselves against doing things for the learners rather than taking steps to enable them to do it for themselves. If truth be told, it feels good to do something for another person and to be acknowledged for that, and that is fine unless it becomes the reason we do it.

In broader advocacy situations, where our association or organization is lobbying for better programs for the learners or for longer access, for example, there is another danger. It is that we will be seen as taking care of our own interests, which are intimately tied to those of the learners. The government may well use these self-interests as an excuse to dismiss advocacy initiatives. One way to protect against this is to form partnerships with other organizations which are less likely to be accused of self-interest in such advocacy. The Canadian Council of Refugees has an excellent track record for immigrant and refugee advocacy. The settlement agencies are also seen as legitimate spokespeople for immigrants and refugees.

We also have to learn, however, that it is both acceptable and necessary to lobby in our own interest. We can do so openly and directly. Other professional associations lobby for better working conditions, job security, and wages. Why, then, do we feel guilty if we do? To some extent, we have to accept accountability for the situation as it is. We have accepted it for a long time. It will only change when we cease to accept it.

Workshop Activity 1

Alone or with a group of colleagues, prepare a set of Best Practice Guidelines that reflect the values you attach to various aspects of your work as an educator. Check your values out with others and see where they differ and where they are the same. Negotiate positions that are agreeable to all.

Workshop Activity 2

Alone or with a group of colleagues, identify the issues that you believe are most central to your professional association at this time. Find out if the association is working on these issues and, if you so choose, if there is a way you can be of assistance to them in doing so.

For Further Reading

Ashworth, Mary. 1985. *Beyond Methodology: Second Language Teaching and the Community*. Cambridge: Cambridge University Press.

This excellent text summarizes the author's many years of experience influencing ESL policy in Canada and teaching others how to do so. She gives good practical suggestions.

CHAPTER 14

Working with Settlement Agencies

Questions to reflect upon:

- What is the role of a settlement agency?
- What is the role of ESL educators in the settlement of newcomers?
- Why has conflict sometimes arisen between these two aspects of newcomer settlement?
- What are some potential benefits to all concerned (teachers, learners, everyone concerned with immigrant settlement) in resolving these conflicts and working more closely and consistently together?
- How can we address the barriers that may have worked against this collaboration in the past?

Settlement Agencies and ESL Providers— Friends or Foes?

While most settlement agencies offer language programs for immigrant newcomers, there has all too often been a tension between the settlement community and the ESL-provider community. These two communities have developed quite separately until very recently when partnerships have begun to take place. This tension has meant that those ESL practitioners or settlement agency staff who did want to cooperate with each other were not always well-received by their counterparts. Government funding policies have also worked to contribute to this tension. Both settlement agencies and ESL providers are working in the interests of immigrant newcomers, and because ESL providers have often been quite ignorant of the services offered by the agencies and the obstacles they encounter in delivering those services, this chapter seeks to provide some information which may enable us to

see settlement workers as our partners rather than our competitors—
and to find new ways of working together.

What is a Settlement Agency?

Anyone working in ESL in an urban centre has some notion of what a
settlement agency is, but what you may not know is the variety of
different mandates which fall under this umbrella. Within a community
that has a large immigrant and refugee population, there may be different types of settlement organizations, each emphasizing different areas.
Also, across the country, mandates shift somewhat in response to
differing regional issues. One theme in common to all of these organizations is immigrant settlement and integration.

Settlement agencies provide counselling, orientation, job training programs, and, in some cases, employment services such as job placement or
referral. The majority of these agencies also provide some sort of language
training program. The strength of settlement agencies is often in the
presence on their staff of large numbers of settled immigrants who offer
not only the languages of their clients, collectively speaking, but also the
understanding which goes with having gone through similar circumstances themselves. While immigrants often feel condescended to at other
service centres, they expect to feel respected at settlement agencies.

In larger centres, settlement agencies often include in their mandate
the desire to promote multiculturalism and anti-racism. This means
that, in addition to serving their clients directly, they are also reaching
out into the community to change public perceptions and attitudes
towards people of other races and cultures. While all of these mandates
are reasonably fundable by various government bodies, the mandate to
serve refugee claimants has been less so, and yet most of these agencies
will also serve refugee claimants, whose needs are often more pressing
than those of their immigrant and sponsored-refugee peers simply because they do not have access to all the other services provided to
landed immigrants.

Human rights is another area in which many of the agencies work.
They respond to some of their clients' experiences of discrimination in
seeking housing or employment, for example. Settlement agencies have
shown leadership in the development of systems to assess foreign
credentials and to enable professionals to get the upgrading they need
to work in their areas of expertise.

Settlement agencies are non-governmental, run by boards, and many
of them are connected to religious affiliations (e.g., Calgary Catholic
Immigration Society, Jewish Family Services, of Ottawa-Carleton, and
the Mennonite Centre for Newcomers, an Edmonton agency). Other
agencies are not connected to religious groups and still others are

centred around the needs of specific groups of immigrant newcomers (e.g., Women Immigrants, in London, Resources for New Canadian Seniors, in Manitoba, and the Immigrant and Visible Minority Women Against Abuse). The larger the community, the greater the possibility of there being highly specific services available. When large numbers of refugees enter a community in the same time period, there are often temporary services established to ease their transition, such as those made available to the waves of Vietnamese refugees in the late seventies.

Ideally, a settlement agency facilitates the integration and inclusion of immigrant newcomers into a receptive and welcoming larger community.

Barriers to the Success of Settlement Agencies

It is indeed a tribute to the staff and boards of successful agencies that they are able to achieve as much as they do, given the numerous obstacles which are taken for granted in the field. The biggest frustration they often face is short-term, limited funding. Settlement agencies learn quickly to do a lot of balancing acts in order to keep services available in spite of sporadic funding. The government may decide, for example, that there are no more Vietnamese people coming in and, therefore, there is no need to provide sustained funding for purposes of their settlement. Meanwhile, Vietnamese people may continue to pour into the agencies seeking everything from translation services to help in dealing with the conflict experienced with their children, as this new Canadianized generation takes on values foreign to the culture of their parents. Settlement agencies have a longstanding history of not turning away anybody who seeks their services, and they maintain that stance by expecting staff to respond to what presents itself rather than to what they are funded to do.

Funding typically comes one year at a time, or less, and must be reapplied for at the end of each funding period. In addition, funding almost always comes from many, many different sources whereas ESL funding is typically from one or two sources. This means that the settlement agencies must commit a great deal of time and energy into applying for funds and demonstrating accountability to many agencies with different reporting structures in place.

One of the problems experienced by agencies is the ongoing battle between federal and provincial policy-makers over who is responsible for what. The federal government constitutionally takes responsibility for the first year of a refugee's or immigrant's presence in Canada, with more services available to government-sponsored refugees. The provincial governments have long argued that the federal government is responsible for settlement, which does not always happen in one year.

The federal LINC (Language Instruction for Newcomers) program was a very positive response to the country's desire for some standardization of language training opportunities across the country. It recognized the special language training needs of women with young children, and seniors. The provinces, for the most part, put more emphasis on language training for employment and simply were not interested, in many cases, in responding to the needs of those not destined for the labour market. This left mothers, who wanted to care for their children at home, with no funding to pursue language training unless they could pay the tuition. This left impoverished seniors, who lacked a community or family to care for them in devastating loneliness and poverty. LINC programs provided a short-term solution for some of these newcomers who were not being served prior to LINC. It is to be hoped that even after the federal government has transferred the responsibility for settlement language training to the provinces, more open options will be preserved. In situations where no one funds the needs of a particular group, settlement agencies have always tried to squeeze these learners in, even if it meant doing so covertly. Interestingly enough, the funders are well aware of these practises and may, in fact, count on them taking place.

Due to the constant scarcity of funds, settlement agencies have learned to live with underpaid staff who have no job security. As a result, if one looks at the staffing of many agencies, one finds an extreme diversity in the qualifications of people working in them. One finds extremely well-qualified people working at an agency because they are committed to doing so, and also very underqualified people working there because they would not find similar work elsewhere due to their lack of qualification. This is particularly true in ESL. Settlement agencies are highly dependent on volunteers for many of the tasks that need doing. It is not uncommon to find volunteers rewarded for their service by being given employment when it becomes available, even though their qualifications may be less than those employees doing the same work in other types of organizations. While institutions typically insist on a teaching certificate and TESL training, for example, settlement agencies seldom, if ever, do. As a result, ESL teachers in settlement agencies, regardless of their qualifications, are typically paid much less for their work than ESL teachers working elsewhere, and herein lies fodder for conflict. ESL teachers who work for agencies resent getting less than they could get elsewhere, and their colleagues working elsewhere resent the wages settlement agency teachers get because it keeps their wages much below the professional norm in other teaching areas.

And this too is not straightforward. Even in situations where the money is available from funders to pay their ESL staff the same wages they would get working elsewhere, agencies are hesitant to do so because of the unfairness it sets up in relation to other staff working side by side with those teachers—the settlement counsellors, for example, whose rates of pay and qualifications are typically much lower than those of their teaching colleagues. In summary, the presence of ESL teachers in settlement agencies has impacted to keep the wages of the ESL profession as a whole low except in those scenarios where such teachers are part of a larger teachers' union.

Whose Role Is Whose?

In that ESL is offered by settlement agencies as well as by school boards, provincial institutions, and private providers, there is a great potential for disagreement over territory. Settlement agencies often argue that it is the job of ESL providers to teach the language and that this ESL instruction does not include settlement education—how to take the bus, how to find a job, how to choose an apartment—which they would regard as their mandate.

ESL providers, on the other hand, argue that language does not exist in a vacuum, that we teach language in order for people to be successful in their lives and that includes all of those things that settlement workers include as their "turf." The problem is further exacerbated when ESL providers are caring individuals who do whatever they can to ease the transition of their students into the new society. Whereas the settlement workers' arguments may have held true when ESL was perceived as the teaching of grammar, vocabulary, and pronunciation, the transition into functional and then communicative competence understandings of language has made that quite impossible. There is no going back to those boxed-in notions of who does what, so we are challenged to find new ways of understanding one another and working together in the interests of both the learners and ourselves.

The Challenge of Collaboration

I was very fortunate in my early days of developing programs as a private provider to have had the support and assistance of staff in one of the settlement agencies in Edmonton, Catholic Social Services. For the first year, we rented meeting room space from them and used their photocopier, paying for what we used. They had not asked for rent but offered us the space free of charge, knowing that we were setting out to provide the same support that they were, just in different venues. Catholic Social Services did not see us as competitors but as partners in a cause.

It therefore came to me as somewhat of a shock when later on, other settlement agencies saw us as competitors and set out to provide the same services we were offering at lower prices, and with lower standards.

Some of these settlement workers even set out to exclude us from associations and to prevent us from having access to the same kinds of funds that they did. One of the favourite weapons used by settlement workers to put down private providers is by referring to them as "for profits," a term which is totally misleading in that any government funding received by private providers is given for non-profit programs. In short, as a private provider, we had to honour the same guidelines and have the same audits taken that they did. Given my previous experience of collaboration with another agency, the outright antagonism from one particular settlement agency was foreign to me and perplexing. Why was it there, and why is it so widespread across the country?

One reason I concluded was that our staff were paid higher wages than theirs, and we could, therefore, attract better-qualified staff. In addition, certain individuals on the agency staff had their own particular reasoning. One of the most vocal antagonists was a man with a union history, and unions, on principle, are antagonistic to private enterprise, seeing it as a threat to their existence unless, of course, the organization is unionized. We all come into new situations with attitudes we have acquired elsewhere, and, just as this man needed to examine the appropriateness of his attitudes in the situation he was in, so too we need to examine and re-examine our own attitudes so that we can understand where others are coming from. If we are going to find ways of working together, we have to learn to appreciate others both for who they are and for what they have to offer the broader picture.

While it is important to stress that many settlement personnel are very collaborative with their ESL counterparts, we must still find ways of understanding those who are not and search for new models by which we can work together because ESL is not going to go away and neither are settlement agencies. Nor, for that matter, are private providers. As ESL providers reading this, you may be saying to yourself, I have never felt any conflict between ESL and settlement agencies. (Perhaps you have never been to a Canadian Congress for Refugees meeting or a gathering of the settlement agencies in a region. If you introduce yourself in either context as an ESL provider, it will not take long to pick up the vibes.) In my experience, the hostility is greater from the agencies towards ESL providers, than in the other direction. On the other hand, ESL providers often pay little attention to settlement workers, and this presents a problem. Not only is such behaviour threatening the settlement workers, but it also indicates a lack of awareness on the part of ESL providers as to the valuable support services the settlement agencies render to our students. We all have some work to do to become better acquainted with and respectful of each other's work.

When our students go to a settlement agency for a particular service, they have the opportunity to become aware of the huge network of services these agencies offer and to become part of the many networks that function within and around the agencies—the ethnic communities and the lobbies, for example. When school is finished for a learner, he often feels set adrift and alone, unless he has found his way into his own ethnic community. Settlement agencies are always having workshops, classes, special training events, and meetings which draw people in. These events help newcomers to know they are participating meaningfully in making things better for themselves and others. Our mandate as ESL providers does not begin to touch any of that.

In addition, we need to have much better communication with our settlement worker friends and colleagues. We need to find out what the agencies are doing and communicate this information to our students. We need to participate in these events ourselves so that we become peers rather than better-paid competitors.

In addition, we can start collaborating as political allies when we advocate for better service for ESL learners. ESL providers and community agencies have a lot of common interests. Our provincial associations need to collaborate with theirs and make joint representations to the policy-makers.

We can try partnering with settlement agencies in jointly providing some programs. This collaboration is already happening very successfully in many places. Such partnerships not only offer more complete services to the learners, but they enable all staff participants to learn about and better understand their colleagues in other contexts. We can also participate as individuals and associations in larger umbrella organizations such as the Canadian Council for Refugees, which addresses issues at the federal and international level. In this way, we add our voices to those already present at that table and at the same time learn a great deal about what is happening in other parts of the country. We can take this information back to our own associations and organizations to improve our programs and services.

Workshop Activity I

Make an appointment to visit a settlement agency near you and spend a day learning about all their different programs. See the obstacles they are up against in providing the services they do and compare their salary-wage levels and working conditions to your own. I am fairly sure you will have a newfound appreciation of the work these dedicated men and women are doing with the same clients we serve in our programs.

CHAPTER 15

Voices and Visions

Questions to reflect upon:

- What is the role of the immigrant in our society?
- What is my role as an ESL professional in our society?
- Who creates the world as it continues to unfold?
- What is the vision of humanity, of the planet, towards which I teach?
- How can I nourish my own ability to envision, and how can I nourish that ability in others I teach?

Voices and Visions: Developing Our Own and Facilitating Such Development for Others

It takes little reach to connect the notion of voice with the teaching of English as a second language because we know that language is first of all about speech. Voice differs from speech in its recognition of the relationship between language and power. To have voice is to have power, to have one's say in the world. In that we are a nation of immigrants, it is strangely ironic that "immigrant" have had so little voice, especially if he or she comes from a non-English-speaking country. When people immigrate from an English-speaking country, we tend not to think of them as immigrants. The word "immigrant" brings different images to different people to be sure, but to some, it brings a sense of *strangeness*, of *poverty*, of *hard work*. This mental picture probably conforms to only a small percentage of the actual immigrants who come each year and yet it persists, even when we know better.

It seems somehow acceptable to some people that the first generation immigrant is in some way a sacrificial offering to the new country. We more easily accept the children of immigrants—who "sound" like us, who look and act like us, who think like us. Many people fear what they do not know or understand, and the result is that for immigrant families who lack other family or community in the new country, there is great loneliness and a sense of exclusion. If an ESL class is about voice, it is also about belonging to a community and having a say in that community.

Vision, on the other hand, is something the majority of us struggle with. If we lack our own sense of voice, and if we do not experience ourselves as powerful, why bother to take the time to envision a better world? What good is a vision if one has no power to do anything about it? Yet without a vision, one of two things happen: we either drift along into the future propelled by forces we have not learned to recognize, or we find ourselves moving into a vision of someone else's dreaming. Hitler's Germany was a good example of the latter. Contemporary society is a good example of the former. We find ourselves often too busy to reflect on the manner in which we live our lives now and too busy to dream of alternatives.

But vision is more than dreaming. Dreaming suggests that which we do not associate with our waking reality. We have no expectations of our dreams, unless we see them as a means of revealing that which is within. Vision, on the other hand, is much more. There is a wonderful dialectic between vision and reality. In the process of envisioning, we have already set into play the forces of realizing that which we have envisioned. Have you ever had the experience of seeing something so clearly in your mind that you were not at all surprised when it one day appeared before you in reality? It has been my experience in life that the envisioning is the hard work and that, once that vision is clear, the rest seems to fall into place—with my cooperation to be sure, but by no means reliant solely on me.

I believe it is very important for those of us charged with the education of immigrant newcomers to be very conscious of the vision towards which we teach. We are the bridge between the old world and the new for these learners. Would we unconsciously lead people into the lonely, prejudiced world of the entry-level immigrant labour market? Or would we support these same people in recognizing what can happen if they enter this world, but at the same time work with them towards finding better employment alternatives, for them and for us as a larger community? I am willing to pay more for my vegetables, garments, and healthcare if I know that the vegetable pickers, garment-makers, and housekeepers of the hospitals are being paid in a manner which respects the value of their labour.

I eagerly invite immigrant newcomers to my home knowing that their stories, their generous spirits, and their differing values have much to teach me, and much to warm my heart. Changing my society begins with changing me in my response to the everyday choices that pop serendipitously into my day. Envisioning begins with a re-examination of the concepts which underlie our practice, and a re-creation of those concepts to be more consistent with the core values of truth, justice, and freedom which unite human beings wherever they live and which honour the divine spark that resides within us all.

Citizenship

Citizenship has long been associated with ESL. Unfortunately, this term has most often been understood to mean preparation for the citizenship examination. Citizenship is a shallow concept in our country and in our education systems as a whole. Citizenship is about belonging to a community and participating fully in that community. It is about having a sense of ownership, pride, and responsibility for everything that goes on in our community. It is about working together with others to identify what kind of community we want and figuring out how we will achieve that vision together in our communities. It is about being accountable for our actions, individually and collectively, and believing that tomorrow can be better than today. It is about healing ourselves and making it possible for others to do likewise.

Indigenous peoples throughout the world have been working steadily to gain the right to reclaim power over their own citizenship. Unlike contemporary Western societies which separate out those who do not conform by sending them to to prisons or psychiatric facilities, old cultures have placed as the highest value the inclusion of each person in the community and have sought to find ways to bring back those who have wandered away from the values of the community. Aboriginal people today are establishing healing circles and developing their own justice systems. They are operating from a vision in which each member of the society matters and each has a necessary role to play for the good of the whole.

Compare this to the vision from which our society receives immigrants into our midst. Whereas North America grew from the presence and hard work of numerous immigrant groups, at some point we seem to have forgotten that and have relegated immigrants to the jobs people born here do not want. Perhaps it happened when the wealthy white colonists decided to import Black slaves to do the hard labour. Perhaps it was when the white government of Canada decided to allow in Chinese immigrants to do the dangerous job of building the national railroad. We have many examples in our histories of racism in action.

In North America today, we have people of every race, colour and language group from all over the world. In Canada, we have official policies of multiculturalism and social justice which give every person equal access to employment, to housing, to participation in government, and to all aspects of citizenship. The fact that we are not yet truly multicultural does not mean that we cannot and must not become so. We have acknowledged in our laws that this is where we want to be. Now comes the hard work of getting there.

What better place to begin the task of being multicultural than in our own ESL classrooms where we have newcomers arriving everyday. For the most part, immigrants and refugees come with open hearts and open minds, expecting the best, hoping for the best. As educators, we begin by questioning our own understandings of what we do and why, and questioning the effect our actions and decisions have on the people in our classrooms. We begin by acknowledging some basic human values: equality, truth, and justice for all. If these are the values inherent to our understanding of what citizenship means, then these are the values that we must expect to find in our own classrooms, and where there is conflict between what we expect to find and what we actually find, this is the place where we must work to understand why that is and to change it. (I can think of several potential research projects in which we could observe and explain the incongruence between the stated values of our classrooms and the experiences of actual teachers and learners within them.)

The Immigrant in North America Today

It is both exciting and disturbing to follow our students into the rest of their lives when they leave the classroom. I have had students, as have many of you, who have gone on to resume brilliant and successful careers as doctors, athletes, ballerinas, real estate agents, musicians and business people, to list a few. I have had others who have, in spite of working in minimum wage jobs themselves, raised children who went on to become lawyers, doctors, concert pianists, dentists, and university professors.

I have also had many learners who, in spite of hard work and good intentions, have worked out their lives in jobs I could not bear to do. Take Chi-Yiau[1], for example, who I taught about seventeen years ago. She was in an ESL literacy class, a cheerful happy woman who had never before been in a classroom of any kind. Since then, she has worked on a mushroom farm cutting mushrooms. Chi-Yiau works seven days a week and does not know, until she arrives, how many hours she will work that day. Sometimes she works six hours a day, but more often it is between three and four hours a day, depending on the orders received by the mushroom farm. She works with other women who speak her language, so her English has shown few changes in all this time. The work is dark, damp, and smelly. The women are paid by

---

1 Her name has been changed to protect her privacy.

the pound and when, as a group, the boss thinks they are working too fast, he cuts the rate per pound.

When Chi-Yiau asked for time off after ten years to go for a holiday to visit her family in her country, she was told that she would have to quit and if there was a job when she got back, she could have it. She cries when she talks about her job. Her husband suffered a workplace injury and has not been able to work for several years now. They get welfare to top off what she makes in her job. Her children work part-time and go to school.

How many of us know people like Chi-Yiau? Because I know her, I hurt for her. I yearn for her to find a better situation, but it is unlikely that she will because she does not believe it is possible. She is happy that her children have been able to go to university and is confident that their lives will be very different from hers. When I buy mushrooms in the store, I think of her and wonder if her fingers cut those mushrooms and got them to me so fresh and so cheap. I wish I could pay more for them and know that the money would go in her pocket.

Our urban communities have left us very disconnected from the means of production of what we consume. We tend not to notice which products come from countries where child labour is exploited and where the environment is destroyed by the improper disposal of industrial chemicals. When we buy a fresh red steak, or a lean, pink porkchop, we tend not to see the animals that have been slaughtered, nor the immigrants who work in the warm, moist stink of the slaughter-house assembly lines. When we stay in a luxurious hotel at an annual conference, we may notice that the maid who cleans our room is an immigrant or other woman of colour, but we never see the grungy, unpainted corridor and the metal side of the mahogany door facing us from the lobby. (One of the benefits of doing English in the Workplace is seeing how immigrants work when they leave our sunny classrooms.)

If we are to make the most of the time we have with ESL learners, we need to increase our awareness as to the larger contexts of their lives. We are not just teaching language in a vacuum; we are teaching language to enable learners to lead happy successful lives. We cannot extricate from our curriculum practise the information they need to do so. Newcomers need to know the labour laws of the province or state where they live. They need to know about the existence of the Human Rights Commissions and/or other bodies designed to protect them from discrimination and harassment in the workplace and in the community. They need to become familiar with WHMIS (Workplace Hazardous Materials Information System), MSDS (Material Safety Data Sheets), and collective agreements. Not only do they need to know how to read this material but they must understand the necessity of doing so if they are working or going to work in jobs where such information is essential to their well-being in the workplace. And if we do not know how to read that information ourselves (and it is not easy!), we need to learn. It matters.

We need to become familiar with what provision there is for immigrant professionals and tradespeople to become credentialed in this country, and where such provision is weak, we can work with our associations to lobby our governments to create bodies which will facilitate such credentialing.

Perhaps most difficult of all, we need to be open to understanding the ways in which our upbringings have distorted the way we see people based on their race, their job, or where they live. I am grateful for the shocking moments when I suddenly become aware of my own stereotypes. It is jarring to learn that the man I saw in the corridor and immediately judged to be a transient using the washroom was in fact a well-known professor who just preferred to have a rather unkempt beard and dress in a very casual fashion when he is not teaching. After each such shocking discovery, I am, at least for a time, more conscious of the need to accept rather than judge each individual. It is hard. We have learned to protect ourselves by judging others and shutting out those who do not conform to our safe definitions, but I have learned that I miss out on a lot when I do that, and I certainly do not do justice to those whom I have judged. By opening ourselves to seeing the beauty in each and every person we meet, regardless of what appears to be, we are allowing the beauty in each person to be free to emerge. When we react to our perceived "uglies," we leave no space for anything else to be in our relationship with the other. To assume instead that everyone is lovable and capable, even if we fail to see these qualities in a person right away, there is a good chance that eventually we will come to see them because we have left such space open.

Furthermore, I find a divine sense of humour at work in my observation that those who I have judged least able to cope with life are often those who surprise me most and teach me most. In other words, when we stop seeing our students as "immigrants" or "students" and see them instead as unique, capable, and beautiful human beings, we will find ourselves pleasantly surprised to see that the learning curve increases as people begin to name their own learning needs and take charge of their own processes, with our support. We do not have to be "the experts." We are experts in our language; the learners are experts in their lives. It is in the authentic dialogue between those two forms of expertise that the best curriculum surfaces for those learners.

Changing Our Stance

The stance of the teacher in the ESL classroom has traditionally been like the stance of most teachers in most classrooms, that of authority figure running the show. The teacher is in charge, and the students expect the teacher to deliver the goods and deal with any problems that arise. The teacher is active and the students are passive, although the teacher would say the learners are actively participating in doing what they are told. The teacher judges the students' progress and, if found wanting, they are potentially removed from the program or obliged to repeat the same content over again.

This traditional stance is replete with problems. I am reminded of what inmates in a federal penitentiary told me when I worked there years ago. They spoke of how hard it was to get out because they had to relearn independence. In prison, they were accustomed to having every decision made for them: when to wake up, when to get up, what to wear, what to eat, where to go at various times of the day. They had virtually no money, although they had a little prison scrip to buy pop and cigarettes. Their choices were minimal and those not controlled by "the Man," as they called the guards, were for the most part controlled by the other inmates, whose code of conduct was absolute and tolerated no deviance. Men had been killed for as small an offense as sitting in the wrong person's place in the cafeteria. Getting out was therefore greeted by long-term inmates with a mixture of joy and terror, for the possibility of re-offense was very high. Ironically these inmates experienced a sense of security in being in an environment they had learned to understand, one in which they did not have to make any decisions. I cannot begin to imagine what it would feel like to be so controlled one moment and experience so many demands the next.

Our immigrant students are not in prison, but in our traditional classrooms they have often been in a very controlled environment, so there are some parallels to be drawn from this situation. I have seen ESL classrooms where the teachers asked all the questions and the students answered. What kind of message does this give? Or, the teachers would make a statement and the students were supposed to ask the question which would result in that answer. This very mechanical kind of teaching, is based on the assumption that students can transfer these mechanisms into real situations. No doubt some can, but these teachers are not looking at the underlying messages in such forms of teaching. There are implications of inherent powerlessness in always doing what one is told and never being asked what one thinks or wants.

When I have discussed participatory forms of education with teachers, some respond by saying that when they ask their students what they want to learn the learners tell them that they are the teachers and that they know best. Those students were like the inmates suddenly released to the outside world. They no longer knew how to use their voices to speak on their own behalf but had accepted someone else deciding everything for them. If those teachers persist and are silent until the learners come up with it, they will find that this expression gets easier each time they ask. But secretly I think the teachers are relieved; it is easier to make the decisions and to believe that the learners really support them in doing so. But is this way better?

I had a colleague for some years who was a natural participatory educator. Herself an immigrant and refugee, she seldom told anyone what to do. She would ask the questions or make the invitation and then wait, as long as it took. Initially, only a few would respond. That was fine. As days and weeks went on, everyone began to participate as they felt comfortable. What she got from her students was so much more than any of the rest of us did. Her students left the program strong, class after class; they were aware, and they were determined to be in charge of their own lives. I saw this woman take students heavily medicated for depression and have them leave twenty weeks later, off the medication, looking twenty years younger, and excitedly embracing life once again.

I envied the ease with which this educator took a different stance in relation to those she taught. She began with the assumption that everyone had something to offer the group, and she approached them with an odd mixture of fierce pride in who she was and yet with humility in relation to the learners. The students, regardless of where they were from, respected and liked her and saw her as a role model. To be sure, her race and her experience as a refugee who had successfully lived in Canada for twenty years were assets in that the learners could identify with her and assumed that she could with them. I know other immigrant teachers who did not adopt the same stance and were neither respected nor liked by the learners, who saw these teachers as having been co-opted by the system which had formerly rejected them. Like the rest of us, immigrant teachers have to be very conscious of retaining a clear sense of their own identities and not acting like they are better than those who have just arrived. This is not always easy, especially for someone who has overcome many obstacles before she or he finally finds employment as a teacher.

For those of us who were born in this country and live in white skin, we do not have those natural assets. We have to find or create our common ground with the learners in some other way. It is not so hard if one genuinely respects the other and accepts him or her as is, without judgment and without condescension. I have found my common ground as a mother, as a parent, as someone who has lost a son to a tragic and unexpected death, and as a human being who respects the newcomer. Community exists when we dwell in our common ground, and when there is little of that, one sometimes has to create it. We do that through storytelling, through laughter and through sharing experiences together, the more challenging or memorable, the better.

A non-authoritarian stance is dependent on the experience of community among a group of people. In community, there is trust; in trust, there is courage and willingness to risk new things. In this environment, a peson is willing to make mistakes and willing to ask questions, to look the fool. In this environment, we can challenge newcomers to work together to support themselves and other immigrants in challenging barriers to their success here. We can inspire them to dream and believe that their dreams can be realized. We can tell them the truth when their dreams are not realistic and support them in redefining visions of the future which are within their reach. And we can make mistakes and not fear their judgment when we do.

Nourishing Our Own Voices and Our Own Ability to Envision

Do you have as much power as you want over your own life? Do you feel that you are completely in charge of creating the life you want to have for yourself and your family? If you say no to one or both of these questions, chances are you can still afford to nourish your own sense of voice and your own ability to envision.

How do we do this, if for years we have done otherwise? For me, the beginning of finding my own voice is learning to listen, to listen first to that still, small voice within me which unerringly knows better than my incomplete logic. That voice speaks itself in silence, and one knows it to be true. It is a voice which never hurts another and certainly does not move to hurt the one in whom it speaks. It is trustworthy and dependable. Perhaps many of you are intimately acquainted with that voice. If you are not, I suggest that you reacquaint yourself with silence. Walk in nature. Listen to the ocean or a river if you are near water. Listen to the wind in the trees. Close your eyes and empty your mind of all the clutter which pushes and pulls you throughout your day. Nature or music can be an invitation to listen to that voice within, the voice which will tell you the truth.

When you begin to hear that voice and know your own truths, you can then become more aware of the words that come from your mouth. You will notice the exaggerations or omissions that make your words more palatable to you or to someone else. You will begin to become aware of the small ways in which you either share power or take it from others. In awareness there is choice. When you have learned to ground your days in the peaceful company of that still, small voice within, you will find yourself with the courage to make the choices that free you from the patterns and injuries of the past and to open yourself up to new ways of being, as a person and as an educator. You will find yourself following intuitions and not needing to justify or explain them to yourself because you "know" that they are right.

When you have learned to listen to the divine spark within yourself, you will find it much easier to listen genuinely to others, not to what they are "saying" but to what they "mean". You will become less dependent on the words and more observant of the body, of the eyes, of the emotions and spirit behind the words. You will begin to understand why others are behaving in ways seemed inexplicable before. It is especially important in trying to communicate with people new to our language that we learn to listen deeply and to respond to the whole person, not just to his or her words. In communicating about things which matter and doing so in a respectful caring manner, we touch the divinity within one another and the language comes in response to the heartfelt invitation. We not only find our own voice anew, but we inspire the voice of the other to surface resonantly.

If you are a busy person who falls into bed exhausted and arises to make a list of what is to be done the next day, ask yourself if you are important enough to yourself to give yourself an hour to just celebrate your being, to listen to your soul? For each of us that might mean something different. It might mean a brisk walk in early morning. It might mean reading an inspiring book which tugs the heartstrings of one's spirit. It might mean dancing in the corridors just because one feels like it. Or it might mean the discipline of daily meditation, or some combination of all these things. Only you can know what your soul needs, but it can only tell you if you listen.

As for vision, this too comes to us in different ways and for some, it is easier than others. I used to do a lot of guided imagery with various groups, and it was always interesting to me when two or three in a group would say, "but I cannot see things." For those who are not visually oriented, use the sense which is strongest. Vision is not just about seeing, in any case, although for many people that is the dominant sense. A fully developed vision is not only seeing in our mind, but also hearing, smelling, feeling, and tasting.

We have to reclaim our imaginations. As children we were born with vivid imaginations. We knew that we could make anything real by simply believing it was so. We made imaginary friends and turned ourselves into kings and queens—and the dog into a dragon. We made stuffed animals sing, dance, and talk to us when we were put to bed early. Then parents and teachers and those pesky, boring adults told us that these imaginings were not real. They made us feel guilty for soaring on wings of fancy, and they kept pulling us back into the present which was generally either boring or terrible in comparison.

All we have to do to reclaim our imaginations is practise. In the beginning, it may be sparse, but if we are diligent in our practise, it will become rich and full. Before we know it, we will experience the synchronicity of finding coincidences that draw into our lives that which we have imagined. There are any number of authors out there who share their experiences in this regard. If you have not encountered any as yet, try reading Deepak Chopra's books. Chopra is a medical doctor who, while trained in Western medicine, had a father trained in ayurvedic medicine (a form of traditional Hindu medicine, which uses naturally based therapies). Chopra writes about health and wholeness, and he has an appreciation of the mystical side of life. Also visit a bookstore and look in the personal development section for an author who speaks to you at this time in your life.

When we have embraced our own personal voices and visions, then we can work effectively with our associates in shaping the vision we want to guide our future as a profession. We can use our newfound voices to lobby for policies which are consistent with those visions, and we can teach learners to do likewise on their own behalf.

Workshop Activity I

Imagine that it is twenty years from now. What would the ideal teaching-learning situation be like for the immigrant newcomer? Describe it in detail: Who is learning what? How are they learning? Where are they? What are they doing? What are you doing? Try to let your mind be as open as possible. Question everything and take nothing for granted. Write down your vision. If possible, share it with others and discuss everyone's visions. What are the common threads? What do those threads have to say about our current practices?

Workshop Activity 2

Imagine yourself to be a student in your class. Put yourself in the chair and see through the student's eyes. How is she or he experiencing the class? How does she feel? What is she thinking? Imagine what she sees in the materials. What kinds of comparisons is she making to other learning opportunities in the past? If you are currently teaching, try sharing your imaginary experience with a class and ask them to comment on the accuracy of your imaginings.

Bibliography

Ashworth, Mary. 1985. *Beyond Methodology: Second Language Teahing and the Community*. Cambridge: Cambridge University Press.

Auerbach, Elsa. 1992. *Making Meaning, Making Change: Participatory Curriculum Development for Adult ESL Literacy*. McHenry, IL: Delta Systems and Washington, DC: Centre for Applied Linguistics.

Barndt, Deborah, Dian Marino, and Ferne Cristall. 1982. *Getting There: Producing Photostories with Immigrant Women*. Toronto: Between the Lines.

Battle, James. 1997. *Overcoming Racism and Achieving Success*. Edmonton: James Battle and Associates.

Bell, Jill. 1991. "Becoming Aware of Literacy". Ph.D. diss., OISE: University of Toronto.

Bell, Jill and Barbara Burnaby. 1984. *A Handbook for ESL Literacy*. Toronto: OISE Press in association with Hodder & Stoughton Limited.

Berdichewsky, Bernardo. 1994. *Racism, Ethnicity, and Multiculturalism*. Vancouver: Future Publications.

Belfiore, Mary Ellen and Barbara Burnaby. 1995. *Teaching English in the Workplace* (2nd Edition) Toronto: Pippen Publishing Ltd. and OISE Press.

CCLOW (Canadian Congress for Learning Opportunities for Women). 1996. *Making Connections: Literacy and EAL Curriculum from a Feminist Perspective*. Toronto: CCLOW.

Chopra, Deepak. 1991. *Unconditional Life: Discovering the Power to Fulfill Your Dreams*. New York: Bantam Press.

Creese, Gillian. 1999. *Contracting Masculinity: Gender, Class and Race in a White-Collar Union, 1944–1994*. Don Mills, ON: Oxford University Press.

Dominelli, L. 1989. "An Uncaring Profession? An Examination of Racism in Social Work," *New Community* 15(3): 391–403.

Freire, Paulo. 1968. *Pedagogy of the Oppressed*. New York: Seabury Press.

Freire, Paulo. 1997. *Pedagogy of Hope: Reliving Pedagogy of the Oppressed*. New York: Continuum.

Gunn, Janet Varner. 1982. *Autobiography: Towards a Poetics of Experience*. Philadelphia: University of Pennsylvania Press.

Hamilton, Mary, et al., Ed. 1994. *Worlds of Literacy*. Clevedon: Multilingual Matters Ltd. and Toronto: OISE.

Henry, Frances, Carol Tator, Winston Mattes, and Tim Rees. 1995. *The Colour of Democracy: Racism in Canadian Society*. Toronto: Harcourt Brace and Co., Canada.

Loney, Martin. 1998. *The Pursuit of Division: Race, Gender, and Preferential Hiring in Canada*. Montreal: McGill and Toronto: Kingston University Press.

McKague, Ormond, Ed. 1991. *Racism in Canada*. Saskatoon: Fifth House Publishers.

Naiman, Joanne. 1997. *How Societies Work: Class, Power and Change in a Canadian Context*. Concord, ON: Irwin Publishing.

Ng, Roxana. 1988. *The Politics of Community Services: Immigrant Women, Class and State*. Toronto: Garamond Press.

Noewen, Henri. 1972. *The Wounded Healer*. New York: Doubleday and Co.

Province of Ontario. 1995. *Commission on Systemic Racism in the Ontario Criminal Justice System*. Toronto: Queen's Printer for Ontario.

Pizanias, Caterina and James S. Frideres, Ed. 1995. *Freedom Within the Margins: The Politics of Exclusion*. Calgary: Detselig Enterprises Ltd.

Sauve, Virginia. 1982. *From One Educator to Another: A Window on Participatory Education*. Edmonton: Grant MacEwen Community College.

Spender, Dale. 1980. *Man Made Language*. London: Routledge-Paul.

Strong-Boag, Veronica, Sherrill Grace, Avigail Eisenberg, and Joan Anderson, Ed. 1998. *Painting the Maple: Essays on Race, Gender and the Construction of Canada*. Vancouver: UBC Press.

Tannen, Deborah. 1990. *You Don"t Understand: Women and Men in Conversation*. New York: Ballantine Books.

Thompson, Jane. 1983. *Learning Liberation: Women's Response to Men's Education*. Great Britain: Croome-Helme.

Wiebe, Rudy with Yvonne Johnson. 1998. *A Stolen Life: A Journey of a Cree Woman*. Toronto: A.A. Knopf Canada.

Index